p. 30 align all
with God.
p. 31, 37, 39, 41, 48, 66,
p. 71 hearing from God.
p. 90 impossible prayers, also 92
p. 94-95 Holy Ground ~~pow~~ prayer
p. 107 Activation of Favor; 109 Favor Confession
p. 121 Heart (Forgiveness)
p. 197 stubborn
p. 234 Angels
p. 252 Daily Prayer of Protection/Power
p. 46 God responds to prayer and Satan
only responds to commands.

Beyond Fearless: How to Remove Every Hindrance From Your Life

Published by New Creations Publishing Co.

7413 Six Forks Rd, Suite 110

Raleigh, NC27615

info@erickajackson.com

Cover Design by Adam Williams, Azhea Entertainment

ISBN-13: 978-0-9745282-1-2

ISBN-10: 0-9745282-1-8

All scriptures are from the New International Version of The Holy Bible unless otherwise indicated.

Dedication

This book is dedicated to every believer who is working in the area of deliverance and healing. Thank you for withstanding the attacks from the enemy and even more so the attacks from believers to whom you had to bring this truth as you walked out God's purpose for your life.

Acknowledgements

There are so many people to thank not just for this book, but for the loving support of my life's work and ministry. To my incredible family, Nathaniel Jackson, Thelma Jackson, Debrena Jackson Gandy, and Nathaniel Jackson, Jr., thank you all for loving me unconditionally and giving me the space to be all of who God intended me to be. He truly picked the best possible family for me.

To my beloved daughter, Kalii, who has sacrificed countless hours of quality time with her mother so this work can get out into the world. I love you and thank you for all you have had to carry and sacrifice on this journey.

Special thanks to Martha McNair, Tonia Scott, Tonya Peace, Ashley Zollicoffer, Erica Jefferson, Shakiria Howie, Jeanette Davis-Loeb and Mona Williams for the countless and selfless hours you have poured into this ministry.

To my wonderful editor, Lakela Atkinson, thank you for your keen eye and your ability to meet my insane deadlines. To Adam Williams, thank you for your patience with all of my design changes until you arrived at the perfect cover for this book.

Thank you also must go to Pastor Jeffery Chapman, Sr. for being a wonderful Pastor who guided my way to preparing for this work. Thank you to the Men of God who cover this ministry, Prophet Micah B. Daniels and Apostle Elijah Forte. Thank you for standing and teaching the absolute truth of Jesus. The best is truly yet to come...

Note: Most of the names of those whose experiences I share have been changed to honor their confidentiality. Their stories are real.

BEYOND FEARLESS

How to Remove *Every* Hindrance From Your Life

By Ericka D. Jackson

Evangelist & Author

*They are to teach my people the difference
between the holy and the common and show
them how to distinguish between the unclean
and the clean.*

-Ezekial 44:23

Table of Contents

Beyond Fearless

Introduction

"Ninety-eight percent of the Body of Christ is oppressed with unclean spirits – from the pulpit down - and they are unaware of it." These are the Words that the Holy Spirit spoke to me in June 2008 and those words catapulted my life to a whole new realm.

It is possible for you to live free from problems, hindrances, and habits that stop you from becoming who God created you to be. It is not only possible, but it is how God created you. Thus it is imperative to walking in the fullness of His vision for your life. When God created you, He had something very specific in mind for you to do and complete in your lifetime. It is possible to become that person without anything holding you back from every good thing that God has provided for you to experience.

Does this sound too good to be true? Well, it's not. That is how God created you and it is time for you to move in the fullness of who you in are in Christ. Yes, you can live problem-free. Yes, you can stop Satan from touching your life. Yes, you can remove every bad habit from your life. Yes, you can live without obstacles slowing you down or stopping you from moving forward. Yes, you can live without lack.

God left a clear blueprint on how to move fully in your gifts and vision. That is what this book lays out for you. We have somehow come to believe that our walk with God is going to be riddled with obstacles and hindrances. Those days are over. This book will show you how to walk into the life God designed for you.

As I was praying for the title of this book, I made lists of potential titles and none of them captured what my spirit knew this book was about. One day as I was working on a project at my computer, the Holy Spirit dropped the title into my mind and heart. I knew instantly that I had it and simply could not think of it on my own. It was perfect – *Beyond Fearless: How To Remove Every Hindrance From Your Life.*

What Is a Hindrance?

A hindrance is defined as *a thing that provides resistance, delay or obstruction to something or someone.* It is an obstacle or barrier that you allow in your life. Hindrances are a result of being disconnected from God's authority and can be removed when you are reunited with the authority God has granted you, in the name of Jesus.

> *Therefore, since we are surrounded by such a great cloud of witnesses, let us throw off everything that hinders and the sin that so easily entangles, and let us run with perseverance the race marked out for us.*
> *- Hebrews 12:1*

It is important to understand that all hindrances are allowed by God. There are many places in the Word that state that God even put certain hindrances in the way of believers to require them to overcome and persist in their walk. God created the entire universe, which includes Satan and his unclean spirits. Satan is the adversary and overcoming the adversary is part of God's process to moving you into your full power, authority, and dominion.

God has revealed a process to me that removes hindrances from your life once and for all. As God brought the title of this book, He was also very specific about the fact that I had to include the Word "every." He left a process so you can live without any barriers, obstacles, obstructions and hesitations. I thank God for allowing me to be the vessel to bring you this important and life-reclaiming work! To God Be the Glory!

Understanding this work requires you to open your mind to the absolute Truth of the Word of God. While this sounds easy, many of us have not been operating in the Truth of the Holy Spirit even though we have attended church for years. The Truth requires you to be willing to admit that you don't know everything there is to know about God. It requires taking off the limitations of who you perceive Jesus to be and to move into a new realm of understanding.

This work was part of the core functions of the ministry of Jesus, yet somehow it has been left out of the day-to-day lives of believers. There is Truth the church has managed to leave out of its teachings and all too often, true deliverance is one of them.

True deliverance has been so edged out of the church that it has become marginalized and considered strange. We talk about Satan and the devil, yet do not understand the workings of the heavenlies or spiritual realm and how they affect our daily lives. We don't understand how clean or unclean spirits work, and therefore, we are living lives detached from the divine nature of Jesus and what it affords us in our daily walk with Him.

While this book may introduce you to unfamiliar concepts, everything I discuss is scriptural and directly from the Holy Spirit to you. This work actually opens up one of the core aspects of Jesus' ministry that every believer should be moving in and expressing daily. When you finish reading this work, you will see that as believers, we have been missing a major key to Kingdom Living.

As I was studying the book of Ezekiel one evening, the scripture I put at the beginning of the book literally sent chills up my spine. The Words literally illuminated from my Bible. *"They are to teach my people the difference between the holy and the common and show them how to distinguish between the unclean and the clean." (Ezekiel 44:23)*

While the Holy Spirit has provided a way for all believers to now access the Holies of Holy and that the only way to God is no longer through the High Priests, this scripture still brilliantly applies and captures my charge in writing this book.

It is both my charge and my prayer that this book moves you from common to holy and from unclean to clean. I pray that this book becomes your pocket resource in truly living the holy life God expects of each of us and shows us how to become clean.

This work may challenge what you currently understand, yet it will be so incredibly obvious that you will be amazed that the Body of Christ has not understood this work on a deeper level. I suppose that God allows His work to unfold at the perfect time which means that the time is now perfect for you to fully grasp the process of cleaning and removing every unclean thing from your heart and spirit - true deliverance.

It's not "woo-woo." Before I fully made the transition from having a business to creating a ministry, I did a lot of corporate speaking and training. The coordinators always told me, "No woo-woo, Ericka." In other words, keep your presentation within the boundaries of intellect and do not enter into spiritual concepts. "Woo-woo" was considered a bit scary to them because they did not understand it.

Until now, the work of deliverance has been "woo-woo" in the church. This perception must change if believers are to fully demonstrate the glory God has set aside for His children.

It is important to also distinguish between hindrances and the things that are God-ordained affliction. Affliction is the process of laying down your life for the life Jesus has for you. It requires that you allow self to die so God can finally use all of you to His glory. Affliction is never easy but always necessary. Hindrances can absolutely be removed from your life 100%, but affliction can only be removed by God.

Afflictions are ordered by God to stretch and grow you to create the capacity within you to carry out His call on your life. Your season of affliction cannot be avoided. Affliction is simply part of the process of walking into your God-given power. God uses the process of affliction to test you to prove yourself worthy of all He has promised you.

While affliction cannot be avoided, it can be moved through with peace, understanding, and little drama. Ideally, you want to move through your season of affliction without any hindrances so you can learn the lessons and it can pass as quickly as possible. You know you are in your season of affliction when you are doing everything right and actively exercising your authority, but seem to have God literally holding things back from you for your learning and growth.

What is Deliverance?

Deliverance is the process of removing unclean or evil spirits from your body. It is a term we have come to use far too loosely in the church. I have heard it associated with everything from a hyped-up sermon that gets you all excited and raises your heart rate to the laying on of hands and being "slain" in the spirit during altar call. We have come to associate the volume of the preacher of a sermon or how long the musicians play with the level of deliverance – as if the louder the preaching gets, the more people are delivered.

When you think of deliverance you may think of certain denominations whose congregants may be gathered at the altar, having hands laid-on them while they are hollering, screaming and laying out on the floor. You may think of the Hollywood-style evil spirits and demons that cause the actor's head to spin around in three-hundred sixty degrees. You may be like Lydia, one of the mothers of a woman I guided through the *Clean Sweep* full deliverance process.

Lydia is a middle-aged woman who grew up all of her life in the church. She is a Deaconess in the church and still had never experienced any deliverance work or understanding of how unclean spirits show up in our lives. She had come to believe that the many challenges and shortcomings in her life were just part of her personality. It took her daughter, Kendra, after attending one of my retreats and being fully freed from all unforgiveness and unclean spirits to be an example of how we are really supposed to live and experience life as Christians.

Kendra was absolutely transformed after the retreat and was sharing her experience with her mother, Lydia. While Lydia did not understand what in the world Kendra was talking about, she did long to be free from the hindrances in her life. She had become a deeply negative person who spent most of her time gossiping and knit-picking her husband because of her lifetime of fear, insecurities and unhealed situations. But, she knew she needed something else.

When Kendra was telling her mother about her experience, Lydia formed a common stereotype in her mind about what I must be like. She took some time to visit my website and was surprised at what she found. In a conversation with Kendra she said, "Oh, Kendra, she is actually pretty." Kendra asked her, "Well, mother, what did you expect?" Lydia answered honestly based on her perception, "I expected her to have on a turban and have something hanging out of her nose." When Lydia shared this with me, I just fell out laughing.

She expected me to be some sort of voodoo priestess or follow some strange form of divination that required me to wear a turban and have either a bone through my nose or a huge nose-piercing of some sort. She also alluded to the fact that she was afraid that her head might spin around and she did not want that. Ha! I assured her that this work is 100% scriptural and based on the work of Jesus Christ as given to me through scripture and the Holy Spirit.

While it sounds funny, the truth is that this is how a majority of the church perceives the work of deliverance and unclean spirits. It is my task to walk you through this in a way that you come to understand it as an integral necessity and requirement to your walk with God. It must become absolutely normal in your life and the life of believers with whom you come in contact.

This work will transform the way you see yourself and the world around you, and you will finally, finally, experience the liberation, freedom, and fruitfulness God promises you in His word.

> *I will sprinkle clean water on you, and you will be clean; I will cleanse you from all your impurities and from all your idols. I will give you a new heart and put a new spirit in you; I will remove from you your heart of stone and give you a heart of flesh.*
>
> *And I will put my Spirit in you and move you to follow my decrees and be careful to keep my laws. You will live in the land I gave your forefathers; you will be my people, and I will be your God. I will save you from all your uncleanness. I will call for the grain and make it plentiful and will not bring famine upon you. I will increase the fruit of the trees and the crops of the field, so that you will no longer suffer disgrace among the nations because of famine. – Ezekiel 36:25 – 30)*

This Word not only applies to Israel, but it is for all believers. Christians have lived in famine far too long and God has been revealing the process that fulfills His Word. This promise can only be fulfilled once you are cleaned, which is what this work is all about.

What is an Unclean Spirit?

As you move forward in clearing a new path for God to manifest in your life, I have to clearly define the difference between an evil spirit, an unclean spirit and a demon. An unclean spirit is an evil spirit that has found its way into the body of a believer (someone who knows Jesus as their Lord and Savior).

While an unclean spirit cannot possess a body that has been dedicated to Jesus, it comes from Satan and is the way he hinders you from completing the work you were created to do to contribute and expand God's Kingdom. A believer cannot be demon-possessed; He can only be oppressed by unclean spirits. Only unbelievers can be demon-possessed because they do not belong to Jesus.

It is important to remember that God created and allows the adversary for the purpose of His glory. He requires you to seek Him to teach you how to move in your authority. His might is demonstrated as we take dominion over every evil, demonic, or unclean spirit in and around your life. It is just part of the process that cannot be shortened or removed from the process of trusting and understanding God.

This book is not about proving whether Satan exists or not. It took only one deliverance session to witness an unclean spirit coming out of a believer, which left no room for debate. It is not about whether or not you believe it. It is fact. Any religion or spiritual doctrine that teaches otherwise is simply not true.

This book will walk you through gaining a new knowledge, understanding and wisdom in identifying and removing every unclean thing from your life. Once your heart and spirit are cleaned, then you will be guided in calling in the clean spirits you need to effectively function and produce good and holy fruit in God's Kingdom.

How to Maximize This Book

When I was 21 years old, I began writing my first book. It was going to be entitled, *Sisters in the Light: Transformation through Self-Love*. While I never completed that book (my daughter made me promise that I would finish it one day soon), it led to a series of wonderful events in my life. I knew that very few people would take me seriously as such a young person writing a book on self-love, so I decided to have a chapter of interviews of seasoned women who would share their process of coming to their place of peace and love within themselves.

One of the incredible women I got the opportunity to interview was Reverend June Gatlin during a summer I spent in California. She had a prophetic gift and just before I turned on the tape recorder (yes, *tape*...recorder), she began to share that this book would be life-changing, one that grandmothers bought for their granddaughters. I believe that she was talking about this book.

While it is me sitting here typing the keys of my laptop, it is not me writing this book. It is God. I am just a mere vessel (Matthew 10:20). My fingers literally fly across the keyboard, and my brain is not engaged in the process what so ever. When I need to recall something God has taught me, He brings it to my remembrance and that is how I know to include it in the writing.

It is my prayer that this book will serve as a guide and reference for your spiritual walk for years to come. I hope it becomes an indispensable resource and one of those books you don't want to be without.

With the vast amount of information in this book, I suggest you take it in by first reading through the book in its entirety, and then taking your time and re-reading the parts that are calling you. If you're like me, when I read a book, I make note of the pages I want to revisit by keeping a list in one of the blank pages in the front of the book. I can always tell a book that I have really enjoyed and learned from because the first blank page I can find in the book has my homemade index. I note the page number and the areas that got my attention so I can locate it quickly when I want to review the information.

I have included many scripture references throughout the writing so you can have the truth of the Word to justify what God has had me share. I recommend that you make note of the scriptures and study them once you have read through the book so they fully support your reading process.

The first part of the book guides you in reestablishing your proper position in the heavenly rank, and the second part of the book is to serve as an index so you can quickly reference what may be hindering your life at various times in your walk with God.

You can index, turn the corners of the pages down, write in the columns or whatever you need to do to remind you where you want to return and study more closely after your initial reading. Once you identify the things that are hindering your life, you can refer back to them as you move to new places in your walk with God.

Each chapter ends with a prayer to serve you in grounding the work in your life and manifesting what it is you need to operate with the seal of the Holy Spirit. Be mindful to stop and pray the prayers after you read each chapter. Refer to them often so they can illuminate your way. At the end of some of the chapters there are also commands that are to be spoken out loud and directly to the enemy.

If you are accustomed to praying silently or whispering in your prayer closet, remember that in order for the commands to be effective you must speak them out loud and in an authoritative tone of voice. Just give warning to those who might hear you praying and keep moving forward. It will bless everyone within ear-shot, I promise.

Put on your seatbelt. It's going to be a great ride!

Beyond Fearless

Chapter One

Twenty Years in the Making

I am always amazed as I look back and see all God was orchestrating on my behalf so this work could come forth. This journey began years ago and culminated when God expanded my gifts, understanding, and purpose into moving in deliverance and healing in the summer of 2008.

As a child, I always had the ability to feel what people felt. It was almost as if I would literally take on their pain. It was a great skill to have as a student leader because it gave me an authentic compassion for those I was chosen to lead. I could easily feel what needed to be done to work with all the different interests in the student body and therefore the teams I led experienced extraordinary results.

This gift was always a challenge in the area of relationships because I would always seem to be the one getting emotionally wounded. Little did I know, this was part of a much larger gift that God would continue to unfold within me for years to come.

This gift of being able to assist and guide people in not only feeling their greatness, but being inspired to take action and move forward is what attracted me to the field of professional personal coaching. While I coached people casually for years, I decided in 2001 that I would make the transition to walking in the fullness of that gift. I was elated to find that they had a term for what I had been experiencing in my coaching sessions – "getting a hit."

For as long as I could remember, I would always be shown the interiors of people's lives. I could look at them and know that they had been molested or at what age something happened to shift their self-concept and esteem. Yet, I could always see how God saw that same person. It wasn't until I found a mentor at my church that I had the Word for my gifts in God's Kingdom – discernment. I have been blessed with an extraordinary ability to discern emotions and spirits. Yes! That was it! It explained so much! It explains why I can feel what someone is dealing with almost the instant he or she walks into a room.

It was after seven years of coaching that I began to grow weary of the coaching process. While clients were always able to get results, I knew there had to be an easier way than managing the challenged areas of their lives. It was time to fulfill the prophetic word I had received so many years before while I was living in Seattle, Washington. A prophet shared with me that God was opening up prophetic and healing mantles in my life. Shortly thereafter, God called me to move my ministry to Raleigh, North Carolina.

After attending a great church, Raleigh North Christian Center in Raleigh, North Carolina and learning under the teachings of Pastor Jeffery Chapman, Sr., he reminded me how to align all areas of my life with God. As a member of this church, my longing for the truth and the will of God in my life increased immeasurably. I literally submerged myself in the things of God.

After three years of this realignment, I was ready to really move forward in manifesting the fullness of my gift and began praying for a new teacher. I needed a teacher whose gift was guiding those who are called to minister to the Body of Christ to gain all they need to fulfill their calling and move in the full expression of God.

When the H.S. is present, 2 things happe.

My ministry was not within the walls of my church of membership. I was called to minister to the Body of Christ and needed more. Then came Apostle Elijah Forte and as they say, the rest was history! After just one class with him, he confirmed what the Holy Spirit had been showing me all along. There is a supernatural level that each and everyone who carries the Holy Spirit can attain. *That* is why I got into coaching in the first place. I wanted to assist people in moving beyond striving for greatness and success, and witness them arrive and thrive *in* their greatness.

In that very first class with Apostle Forte, he shared the pure and unaltered Truth – when the Holy Spirit is present, two things inevitably occur. People are delivered from unclean or evil spirits, and all forms of sickness and disease are healed. He continued to teach that there is always evidence of a move of the Holy Spirit. I could feel my mind and heart shouting for joy and he confirmed that without that evidence, the Holy Spirit was simply not present – no matter how emotional a service became.

As God spoke through him, I was astounded at the fact that we seldom experience the full expression of God – the Holy Spirit – in the Church anymore. It was rare, if ever, that I heard stories of deliverance and healing truly happening. Yes, I heard preachers preaching about it, but I saw no evidence.

When he said that my mouth fell open and at the same time my soul and spirit jumped for joy. I knew that there was so much more, a whole new reality and dimension that God created us to experience. I knew immediately that the absolute Truth God had revealed to Apostle Forte was the next step. He shared what the Holy Spirit revealed to him and I knew that I had found my next level. He was the teacher I had been praying for. I thanked God for two straight days!

That sent me on a quest. At the same time, Tonia, an incredible woman God sent to help my ministry flourish, kept talking about this book she was reading about pigs. She began telling me how this book chronicled the deliverance ministry of a couple, Frank and Ida Mae Hammond. It was this book, *Pigs in The Parlor*, that first deeply resounded with the Holy Spirit within me. I knew with every fiber of my being that this was the next step on my journey to fully manifesting the gifts God placed within me.

The part of this work that became central to my understanding is its teaching on how unclean spirits are expelled. This provided me with enough information to begin to look to the Holy Spirit to lead my way into this most precious work of Jesus, the disciples, and all believers.

I also knew that no matter the teacher whom God's sends, my responsibility is to constantly search the scriptures on my own to confirm and go deeper into the Word. That meant that I also needed to be in prayer for tools and resources to come forth. Within two days of my prayer for more resources, Tonia, who has proven to have been sent from God to provide critical divine connections, visited a church in another city and brought me back the book that provided the breakthrough I was praying for in moving the next level of this work – *How to Try A Spirit: By Their Fruits You Will Know Them* by Mary Garrison (©1976 by Mary Garrison of Christ Camp Ministries, Inc.).

This small 62-paged book initiated the most powerful teaching I could have ever gotten my hands on. It took my understanding of how to identify stronghold spirits to new heights and from that moment on, the work took on a life of its own. When I read that it was the Holy Spirit that schooled her in these teachings, it resonated with the Truth I could feel in my spirit.

Ms. Garrison is a pioneer in this area and I am so grateful that she took the time to listen to the voice of God as he poured in these teachings so she could write and more than 40 years later, her work could find its way into my hands. I pray that this work honors the countless hours of ministry and time spent with God that this work has required of her. I can only imagine all of the individuals she allowed God to use her to free over the past forty-plus years. I also pray that this work is a pure and true representation and continuation of the truth God revealed to her.

Once I began to deeply understand the fruit of unclean spirits and how they manifest in the lives of believers, I also knew why the Body of Christ was not experiencing the fullness of God on a regular basis. Despite the praising, worshipping and teaching that is going on in the church, the church had gotten away from experiencing deliverance and healing. Oh yes, it was time for a whole new reality in God.

I immediately put the Word out to my flock that my work had evolved into a new form and they showed up. I learned more and more with each deliverance session I performed. The Holy Spirit would show me deeper aspects of the process every time He used me to do this work. This book goes beyond any book I have read on this topic, and I pray that it is honorable continuation of the work of every person who moves in a deliverance ministry.

My challenge is to take this core ministry of Jesus' and break it down in a way that it becomes the norm for all Christians, just as it was meant to be. We cannot be whole in Christ without being fully delivered. This book is designed to give you a full understanding and walk you through the entire process to have your heart and spirit cleaned. Then, and only then, can your will become His will and you can move out into the world as all of who Jesus created you to be.

Until you have removed every unclean thing from your heart and spirit, you will not be able to fully hear God and know His path for your life. When I was convening with God one day as He was pouring this work into me, I asked Him, "How bad is it?" He

heart and spirit must be clean.

replied with the same quote I used in the opening line of the book, "Ninety-eight percent of the Body of Christ is oppressed with unclean spirits – from the Pulpit down - and are unaware of it."

"Ninety-eight percent of the Body of Christ is oppressed with unclean spirits – from the Pulpit on down - and are unaware of it."

That means that almost everyone, from the Apostles, Bishops, Pastors, Evangelists, Prophets, Ministers, Elders, and Deacons on down to the congregation are oppressed with unclean spirits and are not aware of it. That makes this work absolutely imperative. If you are to become the person you pray of becoming, you must go through this process. All ninety-eight percent of the Body of Christ, God's Church, *must* experience full deliverance.

It is not until this process of having your heart and spirit cleansed that God will truly allow you to experience His fullness. He promises that He will increase every part of your life, but not until you are clean. He promises that He will bring you into your promised land, the land He set aside for you, but not until you are clean.

He promises that His Church will no longer live in a way that appears to be less prosperous than the sinners of the world. He will increase the fruit of your life so that you will no longer live in disgrace among the nations because you are lacking the things that you need to live. In other words, He will fulfill His Word in you...but not until you are cleaned.

Where Did These Teachings Come From?

I have been amazed at witnessing God formulate this book within me. As each day has gone by, He has added new insights, teachings, and learning. This work goes beyond what I have been able to find in even the Word. I have had to rely solely upon the Holy Spirit for the teaching, understanding, revelation, and wisdom to move in this area.

While this work is 100% based on scripture and the stronghold spirits are clearly identified in the Word, the categorization of them has come directly from the Holy Spirit. This means that you have the ability to recognize it as the Truth of God inside of you. The only two books that God allowed me to read to lay the foundation of this work are *Pigs in the Parlor* by Frank and Ida Mae Hammond and *How to Try A Spirit* by Mary Garrison. Everything else came directly from God. These teachings have all been tried and tested and have proven to be absolutely correct.

I finally understand what my Apostle was sharing one day when He said, "The Bible is all Truth, but all Truth is not in the Bible." Otherwise, there would not have been a need for the Spirit of Truth (the Holy Spirit) to come from Jesus and lead and guide you in the way of all Truth in Him. I just praise God for this work and for leaving within you the ability to recognize and discern the truth.

A PRAYER FOR YOU

Heavenly Father, in the name of Jesus, I thank you for everything you are and everything you have been in my life. I thank you for every challenge and triumph you have allowed me to experience for they have created the character and perseverance to bring me to this moment in which I stand in your perfect will for my life. I thank you for orchestrating all you did so that I may be holding this work in my hands at this time standing ready to move into the fullness of the life you have created me to live.

I thank you for making me the head and not the tail. I thank you for positioning me above and not beneath all things in this world and all things in the spiritual realms. I thank you for the gift of my life and the breath I have in my body because they represent another chance to do Your will and live Your way. I thank you for being my Shepherd and leading me away from temptation and delivering me from evil.

Thank you for opening up Your good treasures and opening up the heavens to give the rain unto my land in this season and blessing all the works of my hands which cause me to lend to nations and not to borrow.

Thank you for restoring all the years the locusts and cankerworms have eaten and opening the windows of Heaven so You can pour down a blessing so large that I shall not even have room enough to receive it, and my life will overflow with blessings.

Thank you, my Lord and Savior, for rebuking the devourer, Satan, in my life so the fruits of my ground burst forth in due season. Thank you for strengthening me so I can not only run, but I can finish the race you have set before me, in Jesus' name. Amen.

Chapter Two

Why Are You Still Unclean?

When God shared with me that ninety-eight percent of all believers – yes, those saved, sanctified and filled with the Holy Ghost – are oppressed with unclean spirits, it blew me away. He also very specifically added to that phrase, "from the pulpit down." Wrapping my understanding around this Truth was a true revelation for me. That meant that with all we thought we knew about God, with all the apostles, prophets, preachers, teachers, evangelists, ninety-eight out of one-hundred of us were still walking around with little to no understanding of this work.

God later revealed to me that without this work, we cannot move into fullness in Him. This leads to the next question I asked God that took months to fully unfold, "Why are we still so unclean?"

Listen very closely to what I am about to share. The only way for unclean spirits to be expelled or leave your body is for them to be commanded to go. And they ONLY respond by name. Prayer, fasting, reading scripture and teaching the Word do not automatically remove unclean spirits, although these practices do greatly assist the process. Absolute Truth can eliminate them over time, but it can take years and years before they may leave entirely. This should be eye-opening to you.

The only way for unclean spirits to be expelled or leave your body is for them to be commanded to go. And they ONLY respond by name or nature.

We have somehow been under the impression that once we pray and ask God to remove them, that they will go. This is not true. God will not remove them for you. He sits back and requires you to ask, seek and knock until you move into the authority, power and dominion He has already granted you. Once you become aware of your authority, power and dominion in His name, you will naturally begin to use His name in all the ways He promised to apply it, including deliverance and healing.

I was being used as a vessel for the deliverance of a lovely young woman named Carol that I had the pleasure of meeting at a retreat of a large local church at which I spoke. But it wasn't until she attended meetings of the Touch and AGree (TAG) Professional Christian Women's Network that I really got the chance to get to know her.

While Carol appeared to be a joyful, optimistic, and well-grounded woman to others, she was struggling with some serious issues. One day, God put a very strong urge to call her on my mind. I literally stopped what I was doing (and I am very focused, so for me to stop what I am doing to pick up the phone and call somebody, I know it is God) and picked up the phone to call her.

I called her with the idea of doing some business together and left a message inquiring. Within minutes Carol returned my call and left me a message saying that she had been really wanting to speak to me. When we connected, she shared that God had just as strongly put me on her mind. She felt strongly that she needed to be delivered and I knew God was instructing me to work with her.

It did not take long for Carol to begin to share just how many challenges she was dealing with. She listed the issues in her life and was so relieved to learn that every issue, from the deep issues of rejection to the anger she was experiencing, was a result of unclean spirits being in her temple (more on that a bit later). My notes on the challenges and hindrances she was facing in her life took the length of an entire sheet of paper.

Her first concern was that she had tried everything and nothing had worked. She visited the altar at her church, had ministers pray for her and experienced the laying on of hands countless times over the years. She even sought psychological help at the suggestion of her pastor and first lady.

She tried different medications for her depression and moodiness. She had read books on deliverance. She had gotten in line many times when guest Evangelists or Prophets were in town preaching; yet nothing seemed to help her, and she was quickly losing hope. However, she was still able to hear the voice of God through all of it and knew to give it a try just one more time.

I had to explain to her that unclean spirits only come out by name and direct command. They do not come out by prayer or even general command. Nor do they come out by The Holy Spirit being present in your temple. She had even prayed with the specific name of a major stronghold spirit in her life and asked God to remove it from her. No results.

Hear me on this – deliverance only happens as a result of direct and specific authoritative command directly to the unclean spirit. The Holy Spirit and unclean spirits can both be dwelling in your temple at the same time – whoa! The presence of the Holy Spirit in your life does not mean that you are clean. The Holy Spirit only fills the places that are unoccupied by unclean spirits, it does not automatically "kick them out" unless it is commanded to do so. I know this is difficult to hear, but it is true.

This is why there are believers who are very oppressed with unclean spirits and are getting minimal results from prayer even if they are "filled" with the Holy Spirit.

The Holy Spirit only fills the places that are unoccupied by unclean spirits. It does not "kick them out."

You still have to speak directly to those unclean stronghold spirits and their fruit in order for them to leave. Then The Holy Spirit fills those places that were left void from the unclean spirits.

Remember, Satan is the prince of the air and he hears, so you must address him directly. That means that it is between you and Satan. God has already given you everything you need in his defeat of Satan. I'll elaborate on more of this in the next chapter.

For now I just need you to fully understand why after all of your praying, fasting, reading and studying scripture, attending church, and countless other expressions of praise, worship and trips to the altar, you have not gotten results or relief from the fruit that unclean spirits have grown in your life. It is the single, largest problem in The Body of Christ right now and it is about to change.

Closing the Gap

As I write these words, I am sharing this work for the first time during one of my monthly conference calls, *Moving Into a New Level of Authority.* One of the Pastors on the call was concerned about the "danger" of teaching people their authority because His assignment in the Body of Christ is to heal, teach, and love those who have been church-hurt. And there are plenty.

He contacted me following the call to openly discuss what he perceived as the danger in the "name it and claim it" teachings. We had a wonderful dialogue and as he was talking to me, he expressed his concern for those he worked with who had tried to walk in their authority and did not get the results they were seeking. He was left to clean up the pieces.

He shared many stories of people that had attempted to cast out sickness from loved ones and yet, they still died. He shared stories of a mother who did everything right by raising her son in the church and yet, her son still hanged himself and ended his short and tormented life.

He shared stories of witnessing and having to work with hundreds of fervent believers, who were long-standing Christians, yet were still struggling financially, spiritually, physically, and emotionally. They had been deeply let down and broken in their attempts to move in their authority, and he was left to clean up the pieces. He jokingly said that if it was not for the church and how it kept destroying Christians, he would have no ministry.

He asked the very important question, "'What happens when walking in your authority doesn't work and how do you deal with the aftermath?'" I have learned to listen and allow the Holy Spirit to speak through me. I clearly heard the Holy Spirit tell me that the problem lies in our lack of understanding of the stronghold spirits and how to recognize them in our lives and a lack of belief.

Three things must be in full alignment in order to keep Satan at bay in your life. You must know your true position in Christ, you must know the stronghold spirit and its fruit by name, and you must speak with bold authority. Because they only respond by name or nature, if you do not have all three aspects lined up, you will not get results. Because many believers are unaware of this,

Satan continues to run amuck creating havoc, destruction and death everywhere he has unknowingly been allowed to touch.

The Holy Spirit also told me to tell this pastor that there was a way to close this gap between what the Word of God promises, and the reality of a majority of the lives of believers. There is a way to get every hindrance out of your life. There is a way to be proactive and take your position over Satan. After doing so, he has to flee from your life. This work shares the process to closing the gap and heal the disappointment that comes when you are trusting God and still experiencing the loss of loved ones, struggle, and destruction. Hallelujah!

A PRAYER FOR YOU

Father God, in the name of Jesus, open my spiritual eyes so that I can see and open my spiritual ears that I can hear you and your Truth. Lord, please forgive me for falling short of your grace and for any area of my life in which I have not represented you as the forgiving, loving, abundant God that You are. Lord, forgive me for any word I have ever spoken that has created strife, limitation, division, or pain in my life. Forgive me for not fully seeking and understanding the power You have granted me through the name of Jesus.

I present myself as a living sacrifice, whole and acceptable in Your sight. Lord, empty me of myself and fill me with Your Word and Your ways so that I will live out the fullness of your power and righteousness in every aspect of my life.

Today, I put down and turn away from the things that come out of my heart and mouth that defile me. I turn away from evil thoughts and pick up the life you have for me. No more shall I shrink away from or minimize Your power within me. Lord, I confess that I have been playing small in my life and I have not fully embraced and obeyed the instructions you have given me to go forth, produce good fruit, and multiply.

Lord, I no longer bury the talents, gifts, and abilities you have blessed me with; but from this day forward, I share them with the world, so that I can give you all of the glory. In Jesus' name. Amen.

Chapter Three

How to Get the Devil Off of Your Heels

As I was preparing for my *Moving The Mountain of Money* workshop a couple of months ago, I received a call from Megan, one of the people who had paid her deposit to attend.

She had a very demanding job that kept her working hours she did not like. She was scheduled to work on the Saturday of the workshop, and was feeling discouraged because her boss was adamantly telling her that she could not get the day off; also, none of her coworkers would fill in for her. She decided to give me a call and let me know what was going on with her situation.

The moment I picked up the phone and heard Megan's voice, I knew that something had happened to attempt to derail her from coming to the workshop. This workshop is an amazing process that walks believers through getting money back into submission, and shows them how to call forth and create money to live out the fullness of God's vision for their lives. Megan was feeling stuck around her finances and knew that she really needed to be at this workshop.

"Good morning, this is Ericka," I answered as I always do. "Hi, Ericka, this is Megan. I tell you, the devil is really on my heels." I replied by asking, "Do you know how to get him off?" Silence. I knew I had asked her a question she had never been asked before. After several moments of silence, she replied, "Yes, pray, right?"

"No. The devil does not respond to prayer," I shared and continued, "Only God responds to prayer. The devil only responds to command." I continued to share with Megan that she has authority over Satan and all of his adversaries. I reminded her that every unclean spirit that Satan sends her way must obey her command in the name of Jesus. Silence again.

The devil does not respond to prayer," I shared and continued, "Only God responds to prayer."

I continued to share that it was just unclean spirits within her boss acting out and they were subject to her. I began to walk her through what to say to these unclean spirits and how to cast them down from manifesting in her presence. She immediately applied the teaching to her boss and co-workers.

I told her to decide that she would be at the workshop and not to allow herself to think or say anything other than the outcome she desired. I told her with absolute certainty that it would work because it had to. And it did. She was at the workshop and had great breakthroughs that have led to her transfer to another department, where she can have the weekend time off she needed to be able to operate in her life's calling, as a massage therapist that God uses to heal people.

Most believers do not know how to get the devil off of their heels because they are unaware that through Jesus, they have dominion over Satan. I can't tell you how many times I have heard entire sermons on the devil taught in a way that presents God and Satan as seemingly powerful forces that are in a tug-of-war for your life.

Nor can I count just how many times I have heard faithful believers share their challenges with dealing with the devil, as if those challenges are just something they have to hold on through and be victimized by. This is just not true and it is time to remember the power over Satan that Jesus already established.

I was speaking at a retreat with the African Methodist Episcopal Church's presiding elder of the 5th District, who is a retired Los Angeles police officer. As she spoke, she shared that she had a love of wrestling when she was younger before realizing that the wrestling matches were staged, and the winner had already been decided.

In this same way, the battle between God and Satan has already been decided. God knows it. Satan knows it. Believers are the only ones who do not seem to know it and still walk through life acting as if Satan actually has power in our lives. This is simply not true.

How Did The Devil Get In?

Anytime I mention the Word, "deliverance," most Christians get nervous because the topic has been so misunderstood. I often hear people respond, "You better be careful moving at that level." The Truth is that it is the level at which all believers are called to move, but have not been taught properly about it.

Once you have a clear understanding of your heavenly rank or position through Christ Jesus, you have nothing to worry about. All demons, devils, and evil spirits are subject to you and must obey when you speak the name of Jesus. They cannot harm you unless you forget that you have dominion over them through Jesus.

The devil cannot move without your permission. You are giving him permission whether or not you are aware of it. I remember one day when I was on a live radio show. We were discussing fear, and the hostess began to talk about how the devil comes in and attempts to destroy your relationships. She said it as if it were the norm and the listening audience just had to get used to it.

Not so! Satan can only enter your life through doorways that you leave open.

Satan can only enter your life through doorways that you leave open.

You unknowingly give Satan legal right to your life by speaking words other than what the Word says about you and your life. You also open the door to Satan by speaking death or negativity over things and people with your tongue, by not knowing and understanding how to move in your authority, and through unrepented sin.

Don't get me wrong and think that the spiritual war that wages for your soul is not serious, because it is. Satan will go to great lengths to stop you from realizing who you are in Jesus. He does everything in his very limited power to keep you deceived and as far away as possible from the Truth of who you really are. The moment you realize who you really are and how powerless he really is, he is doomed.

Anytime you are taking an aspect of your life back from Satan, remember the analogy that the match has already been staged for your victory.

How Do You Get the Devil Out?

Unclean spirits do not come out only by praise and worship. They do not come out by prayer or asking God to remove them. They do not come out only by reading and studying the Word. They only come out by applying the absolute truth of God and speaking to them directly by name, or by their nature (I go into more detail about this in Chapter Nine).

Unclean spirits only come out by applying the absolute truth of God and speaking to them directly by name or nature.

I know that this can really challenge you, but it is true. On a ministry trip back to my former church, First AME in Seattle, WA, this truth literally created an uproar with the women at the retreat at which I was teaching.

One of the mothers of the church, whom I love dearly and worked with for years as a Sunday school teacher, stood up and completely rejected that she should be speaking directly to Satan and his unclean spirits. She said that she would leave that up to God and He would take care of it. I just stood there and said nothing because there was no need to defend the Word of God. It will defend itself. I knew it was only God keeping my mouth closed because my natural instinct would have been to go into teaching mode.

There was no way that I could explain and have her hear through her own spirits of fear and haughtiness (sorry, but it is so true. There are few of us who are not carrying these unclean spirits) the countless stories of people God had sent to me who have experienced deliverance services in their church services, who loved the Lord, were "filled" with the Holy Spirit, and have been walking on God's path most of their lives but who had not actually been delivered at all. This is because in everything they had attempted, no one guided them through the required forgiveness work and actually spoke directly to the stronghold spirits and their fruit by name.

She gave the example that even the archangel did not speak directly to Satan and left that to God (Jude 1:9). I continued to stand there and began praying for the Holy Spirit to uncover the ears and eyes of his people so they can recognize the Truth. She became open to learning more and told me that she was beginning to understand what I was sharing. She ended up giving me a hug after the workshop and purchasing some of my products.

I went back to my hotel and checked the scripture so I could further address this on the second day of the workshop. Remember that in the Old Testament, Satan had not yet been defeated by the death and resurrection of Jesus and therefore there was no power other than God over him at that point. He had to have the Lord rebuke him in lieu of speaking directly to Satan.

I actually had to check with Apostle Forte on this one because the scripture also says that Jesus was made just below the angels (Hebrews 2:7-8). I needed to fully understand exactly where believers ranked in the heavenly scheme of things. This is critical to understanding your power, dominion, and authority over Satan.

As I was asking Apostle Forte, I heard the Holy Spirit say, "It is in the Word *made*." I knew that there was something I was missing. Apostle Forte's answer cleared it up for me. He told me that before Jesus our heavenly position was under the angels; after Jesus, it was placed above the angels.

That was it! When Jesus died, was buried, and was resurrected, God placed Him at His right hand. That means that through Jesus, believers are positioned at the right hand of God.

It is the death and resurrection of Jesus that gives you the power over Satan. Without the heavenly rank and position that you were granted through Jesus, you would be powerless. According to Ephesians 1:7 and 2:6, you are positioned above the Angels and therefore can speak directly to Satan, who must obey in Jesus' name.

Why Hasn't Deliverance Worked In The Past?

We have come to mistakenly use the Word "deliverance" in the place of "enlighten" in the church. We hear prayers to God that might resemble something like, "Lord, we pray for deliverance in areas that we need to be delivered and set free. I pray that no one will leave without receiving whatever it is that you have for them to receive today." Deliverance is when an unclean spirit comes out of the temple of a believer. Anything less is not true deliverance.

Deliverance is when an unclean spirit comes out of the temple or body of a believer. Anything is not true deliverance.

Yet, at no point in the service are the unclean spirits actually directly addressed, called by name and cast out. Or the truth of the teaching gets covered up with the many other things that take place during a traditional church service, and the Truth cannot permeate the presence of the unclean spirits in the congregants so they can be set free.

The other reason that you may not have experienced true deliverance even with all of the praying and seeking God that you may have done, is that you have to have a clear understanding of the stronghold spirits and their fruits, or you will not get results. If fruit of a stronghold spirit is mistaken for a spirit, only the fruit is cast out, not the stronghold spirit that created the fruit.

Therefore, you will only experience freedom from a manifestation of an unclean spirit for only a season and then it grows back because the stronghold spirit was not bound and cast out. I explain more of this later in the book.

It is also paramount to understand that deliverance can only happen once you have released all unforgiveness. If you cast out unclean spirits and unforgiveness still remains, the unclean will not fully be expelled.

Another reason that we so often mention deliverance, but fail to experience it, is because God is just really opening up His church to experience it on a mass level. There have been pockets of deliverance ministers, but not nearly enough to reach the masses of believers. When believers are taught how to cast out unclean spirits and lay hands on the sick and they will be well, then the Kingdom will gain the power in which God created it.

I pray with the help of this book, my online learning institute, and the ministers God is bringing me to train up, will truly take this work to a new place. It is also my prayer that all of the ministers that have been moving in total deliverance will come together and allow the synergy of our work to transform the Kingdom, in Jesus' name. Amen.

A PRAYER FOR YOU

Father, in the name of Jesus, today I forcefully take hold of the Kingdom of Heaven. I come boldly to the throne of grace, so I can obtain your mercy and grace to help in my times of need. I ask that Your Word of truth quickly, powerfully and sharply divide my soul and spirit and separate what is of You and what is of the enemy, in Jesus' name.

Bring to my awareness every unclean thing that has found its way into my life, and show me the way to rid myself of each and every one of these unclean things so I live the life you predestined me to live before you even placed me in my mother's womb.

As a result of this work, I rise up and take the reigns You have left me to move in the dominion over my life, my circumstances, this world, and the law. I crucify the sinful nature with its passions and desires and give myself over to live in the Spirit.

I put down every unclean spirit that has unknowingly or knowingly produced unclean fruit in my life. I stand firm in the freedom of Jesus Christ, and will no longer allow myself to be burdened by the yoke of sin. I allow nothing or no one to keep me from obeying the truth and cutting in on the good race I have been running.

I fully embody the Holy Spirit and its fruit, and engraft myself to the truthful Word of God so I am good ground with good soil where the Word of Truth and works of God can be planted, grow, and produce a good crop that multiplies thirty, sixty and a hundred-fold. The knowledge of the secrets of the kingdom of heaven that has been given to me are opening up in me right now so I can lead those God sends to me, in Jesus' name. Amen.

Chapter Four

Remembering Who You Are

I grew up in the church, searched the world religions to explore my questions about God, came back home to the church, and still was not ever taught who I was in Jesus. As I travel to different churches, I am amazed just how ignorant believers are about who they are in Jesus. We know who Jesus is, we just have not been taught who we are *in* Jesus.

There are two aspects of knowing who you are in Christ: your divine aspect and your human aspect. As I dug deeper in the Word and began to ask God to show me the higher things of Him, I realized that I had spent my entire life learning and focusing on the human aspect of myself. I had not yet been taught the divine aspect of who I am and what I now have access to through in Jesus.

I first realized this as I sat week after week, sermon after sermon, and Bible study after Bible study in my church in Raleigh. Yes, the information and facts of the Word were continuing to be taught, but the truth of who I am through Jesus was not at the level I needed them to be to fulfill my calling. At first, these teachings served as a powerful way to realign my life with God and to get the sin out of my life.

He taught well on how to live my natural life, yet I was longing to understand the higher mysteries and wonders of God. I was thirsty to understand how to walk in the fullness of my calling, which was outside the walls of my church. I knew I was called to the Kingdom and was feeling confined in my church as there were few teachings on how to apply my gifts in the world.

It was time to move into the fulfillment of the prophecy that was spoken over my life by Prophet Bryant K. Osborne, who I met in Seattle, Washington before moving to Raleigh. On one particular day five years ago, I had grown weary in well-doing and was at my breaking point. I felt like I simply could not go on doing this work and unless something miraculous happened *that* day, I was going to throw in the towel, get a job, and move this work to the back burner of my life. It was feeling too hard that day.

It was that day for the second time in five years that God sent Bryant "BK" Osborne to deliver a word of prophecy to me. He said, "God is opening up a prophetic mantle and a healing mantle in your life." I was already beginning to walk in the prophetic, so I knew that his words were confirmation, but the healing mantle had not yet opened up. That night I studied the Word "mantle" so I could fully grasp what he shared with me. I came to understand that his words really meant the full mantle of being a supernatural healer and vessel for God's miraculous spiritual, physical, emotional, and mental healing.

Years later, this prophetic word continued to unfold in my ministry and in communion with The Holy Spirit. The next piece of deeper understanding came during the very first class I attended with Apostle Forte. He was teaching from Ephesians 1:19 about how God placed all things under Jesus' feet.

> *That power is like the working of his mighty strength, which he exerted in Christ when he raised him from the dead and seated him at his right had in the heavenly realms, far above all rule and authority, power and dominion, and every title that can be given, not only the present age but also in the one to come. And God placed all things under his feet and appointed him to be the head over everything for the*

church, which is his body, the fullness of him who
fills everything in every way.

Yes, I was familiar with that. Then, he continued in Ephesians 2:6 that so clearly stated, "And God raised us up with Christ and seated us with him in the heavenly realms in Christ Jesus, in order that in the coming ages he might show the incomparable riches of his grace, expressing in his kindness to us in Christ Jesus." Did you catch it? Did you see it? Or did you miss it as I had so many times. Let me show you again.

And God raised us up with Christ and seated us with
him in the heavenly realms in Christ Jesus...

If God raised you (the Church or the Body of Christ) up and seated you at the right hand of Jesus, then that means that your rightful place is in the heavenly realm and that all things are under your feet. In other words, you have power, dominion, and authority over all things of the spiritual world *and* all things in the natural realm.

Yet, I was living like things had control over me because I had not received the revelation of this Word from God. Even in having been working my Kingdom assignment full-time for almost seven years, I was still not operating as if I had all things under my feet – including Satan. I was still far too affected by the people and the things of this world. It was that day that I began to remember who I was in Jesus, and it is time for you to remember.

At the beginning of the year, I was invited to speak at a women's retreat in the African Methodist Episcopal (AME) system. As I heard from the Holy Spirit as to what He would have me teach, he commanded me to teach that Satan had already been defeated and our true rank in the heavenly realm. Before I moved from Seattle, I attended an AME church and was very familiar with the limitations of experiencing God that are taught by that church system.

I trusted God and prayed that each of the presenters would line up with the truth of the Word, as I was the only minister coming to speak from outside of the AME system. The retreat coordinator had a conference call early one morning in preparation for the retreat and each of us shared a bit about what we would be teaching.

My teaching directly followed a minister I knew but had never discussed her understanding of the rank of believers in the heavenly realm. She shared only that she would be teaching the women how to go to war against the enemy and would be dressing up in a way that illustrated her point. I remember thinking, "Lord, I pray that everything we teach lines up with the truth that Satan has already been defeated and the war has already been won."

I remained in a state of prayer as the morning of the retreat came. She did teach that there was a war and that it had already been rigged for our victory. I thought, "Whew! Thank you, God!" It was the perfect segue into what God was having me teach. As God would also have it, she spoke briefly that there is a realm between Heaven and earth in which evil dwells and a war is raging. My heart jumped for joy in my chest! Talk about the perfect set-up!

I was able to build upon the Truth that she taught seamlessly. I begin by sharing that the war had not only been rigged, but it had already been won (which meant that there really was no war at all). I was able to share that the realm she was talking about that exists between the earth and heaven is actually in submission to believers. Did you catch that? Satan is subject to your power in Christ Jesus. Satan only submits to the name of Jesus.

Satan is subject to your power in Christ Jesus.
He only submits to the name of Jesus.

The Adversary

If someone would have told me years ago that I would be moving in deliverance and writing a book with a section on Satan, I would have gotten a good laugh and would have never believed it. With all of my work being about moving forward and living the life God created you to live, I never would have thought that part of that process requires gaining a clear understanding as to how Satan operates and how to keep him at bay.

I remember laughing to myself when I was 17 years old and Ms. Pat Hawthorne, my creative writing teacher at Timberline High School, told me that she thought I would be a minister. She explained that she knew that I would do something where I would influence a lot of people and stated with certainty that I would become a minister. I stood there thinking, "No way would I ever be a Pastor," without understanding that ministering did not mean that I would be a pastor.

I slowly walked back to my desk and shared it with my best male friend, Scott, and we got a good laugh from that one. I laughed then, yet here I am twenty years later ministering and knowing that I am right where I am supposed to be. If I ever get the chance to see Ms. Hawthorne again, I look forward to sharing this with her.

Your Real Self

God created you above all things and gave you all power through Christ Jesus. God granted you literal power over death itself. All spirits are subject to you (Luke 10:20). He gave you the power to speak life or death with your tongue (Proverbs 18:21). Through Jesus, your actual position is above this world at His right hand in the heavenly realm.

Yes, you have a human nature, but you first have a divine nature and you are not of this world (John 17:14); you are in this world to subdue it (Genesis 1:28). All things were created to be subject to you, which means that they must submit and are to obey your words.

Jesus defeated the devil and his works (1 John 3:8). Satan knows it and literally preys on our lack of knowing that he has already been defeated. All of this means that Satan is subject to Jesus and you sit at the right hand of Jesus. I repeat – Satan is subject to Jesus through you. This understanding is paramount to removing every hindrance from your life.

Hindrances are from the devil. Hindrances are things that are placed in your way to stop, deter or abort the path you are on for God. Once you fully grasp that Satan is subject to you when you speak in the name of Jesus and that he has been fully overcome, you realize that he then must listen to your command and respond accordingly. The problem is that we aren't commanding, we are just allowing Satan to run rampant and unchecked in our lives.

I was just on the phone with the husband of a woman I had guided through *A Clean Sweep*. She wanted me to speak with her husband to hear just how transformed she has been since our work together. He began to share with me the many improvements he has seen in his wife since she spoke with me. Then he said, "Satan is just going to get in our marriage. We just have to remain together and work through it." I had to correct him because his statement held one of the biggest lies that has been allowed to remain in the church.

Satan cannot just come and go in your life. He is subject to you and he must - 100% of the time – follow your command. I reminded Lydia's husband that as the head of household, he really needs to close the doors in his life and in the marriage to which Satan has gained access.

Yet, a vast majority of Christians live defeated lives. We experience sickness, depression, financial struggle, stress, failure and many other things that are not from God. This must stop immediately. We can no longer say we represent Christ and live defeated, sub-par lives that make sinners prefer what the world has to offer when they see the fruit of our lives. This stops today. It is time for you to understand the revelation of who you really are, not who you have become.

Beginning today, you are leaving the lie of your past life behind. You are putting down the life that you created for yourself and picking up the life that Jesus created for you to live. Enough. Beginning today, all those who profess that Jesus Christ is their Lord and Savior will live lives that are the example of what is possible when you are co-heir (Romans 8:17) with Christ.

The Real You: Unraveling the Braid

In your life, you are not really who you have come to believe yourself to be. No matter how successful you may already be or how spiritual you are, God has created you to be more powerful. Yet, far too many of our lives have become a braid and not the truth. A braid has three strands and these strands are wrapped together one over another until they form a stronger and seemingly complete whole.

This braid consists of one strand that represents who God created you to be – your real Self. The second strand of the braid consists of your emotional pain from your past. The third strand of your braid represents the unclean spirits that you have come to believe are a natural part of who you are.

You must take your braid apart and eliminate the parts of you that are not who God actually intended you to be. You were born to live with no emotional pain or unclean spirits. Yet, without carrying the emotional baggage from your past and the fruit of unclean spirits that you have unknowingly come to think of as parts of your character or personality, you may not know how much of "you" that leaves.

As I was learning of the many, many manifestations of unclean fruit in my life, I was blown away to see how many of those fruits I had sincerely come to know and believe to be part of my personality. One day during my studies, I just stopped and asked the Lord, "If all of these things are not the real me, then who am I?"

He flashed two scriptures in my head and said that anything other than what is in these two scriptures is not of Him. The scriptures were Galatians 5:22 in which God shares the fruit or evidence of the Holy Spirit in your life: love, joy, peace, patience, kindness, goodness, faithfulness, gentleness and self-control. The other scripture was Philippians 4:8 that teaches:

> *"Whatever is true, whatever is noble, whatever is right, whatever is pure, whatever is lovely, whatever is admirable – if anything is excellent or praiseworthy – think about such things."*

God was telling me that if it was not one of these things, then it was not who I naturally am in Him.

Yes, you get to keep the characteristics that are at the core of your being, just not the mess that you have come to carry over the years. We often say of someone who just seems to be off or have bad habits, "That's just the way they are," or "That is just how Johnny is."

This is not so if Johnny is a believer. Those bad habits and characteristics are not who God created him to be, they are what the world has molded him into. It is time to uncover who you really are and begin to live life from the truth of who you are and not the lies that the world wants you to believe so you never realized your greatness.

You can be saved, sanctified, love the Lord, and still have a heart of stone. You can even serve in the church, preach in the pulpit, direct the choir, be married to a pastor and still have a heart of stone. You can be someone who reads the Word, prays daily, is working on your Kingdom assignment, and still have a hardened heart. You can even be in a seemingly good marriage in which both you and your spouse are serving God, and still carry around hurt and pain if you have not done this work.

You may have even come to believe that the hurt and wounds from your past are just something you have to carry around and bear. This is not the truth.

You were created to have a clean heart – a heart free from all hurt, anger, pain, bitterness, wounds and impurities. For now, just know it is possible. I will walk you through the process of actually cleaning your heart in Chapter Four.

For now, you have got to begin opening your mind up to the possibility that you can be free in your heart, no matter what you have been through in your past. You can live a life of pure joy, no matter how many times you have been hurt, betrayed, wronged, or violated.

Begin to imagine your life with no emotional pain from your past. Imagine your heart being whole and free from any past hurts or wounds. This work will take you there. No more anger. No more bitterness. No more having to feel like you have to guard your heart from anyone being able to hurt you. God left you a process of literally putting the pieces of your heart back together again and living with a clean heart, a heart of flesh and not of stone.

The Breakthrough Coach in me has to take advantage of this coaching moment and help you find your own answers and path to living with a clean heart. Take a few minutes to explore these questions and write down your answers. If you are someone who does not like to write in your books, get out a piece of paper and write down these questions and your answers. Answer the following questions, even if you think you have already done this work before:

What would you be like with no emotional pain in your heart?

_____
_____
_____
_____
_____
_____
_____

How would you move through your world differently?

_____
_____
_____
_____
_____
_____

Would you feel differently? How?

_____
_____
_____
_____
_____

What would you do or say differently?

_____

_____

_____

_____

_____

_____

Taking Your Rightful Place in Jesus

The Word clearly tells you that you have been given all power through Jesus. Hebrews 2:14 tells you that Jesus came to destroy the devil. I Colossians: 15 teaches how Jesus "disarmed the powers and authorities and made a public spectacle of them, triumphing over them at the cross." If we missed those verses or have never heard a sermon on the Truth of your power over Satan, the Word brings it home in I John 3:8 as it says, "The reason the Son of God appeared was to destroy the devil's work."

Jesus himself tells us in Luke 10:19 – 20 that he saw Satan fall like lightning from Heaven. He continues to declare that He has "given you authority to trample on snakes and scorpions and to overcome all the power of the enemy; nothing will harm you." The snake this passage refers to is Satan; the scorpions are evil spirits. One of the main reasons God brought Jesus was so you can take your rightful place over Satan, who has already been defeated.

You already know that when you accepted Jesus Christ as your Lord and Savior, He forgave your sins. But, do you know *how* He atoned for your sins? Because Satan rules sin. When Jesus died, He atoned for your sins because He defeated Satan, the ruler of sin. That is why it is only through Jesus that you can be cleansed of your sins and live a life above sin. When Jesus died on the cross, He completed the work of defeating Satan and gave you access to the divine nature of God through His Holy Spirit.

Satan cannot touch you without your permission. He can only enter through open "doors" in your life. You give him permission to enter through sin and using your tongue to speak ungodly things. Even without you being aware of it, the sin of your parents may have opened doors to Satan. I will share more about this as I cover the stronghold spirits and the fruit they produce in your life. I will also share how the doors got opened in your life.

You are The Temple of God

One of the keys to understanding how the spirit realm works is to first remember that you are the temple of God (I Corinthians 3:16). You are the only temple that was made by God and not the hands of man (Acts 17:24). You are God's sacred living quarters in which He dwells, and through which, He changes the world. You are God's most sacred creation. That is why He gave you all power and made everything yours (Luke 3:21).

Yet, when you think of God, you may think of Him as coming from the outside of you, when indeed He comes from inside of you. He does not "drop by your life" as you may have come to believe. In I Corinthians 3:16, the Apostle Paul challenges the Corinthians with the question, "Don't you know that you yourselves are God's temple and that God's Spirit in you? If anyone destroys God's temple, God will destroy him; for God's temple is sacred, and you are that temple."

The Kingdom of God is Within You

How many times have you been in a church service and heard whoever was standing in the pulpit ask God to stop by? As if God is a UPS man who is going to come in from the outside and bring a package of salvation, deliverance, and healing only on some days and pass by to other churches on other days. How often have you prayed in your time with God that He show up in your life as if His power is outside of you?

I attended church for the first 36 years of my life before I truly understood that I am the temple of God and His Kingdom resides within me (Luke 17:21). The address of God is your address. You are the chance of those in your life to witness God. He works through you and I.

He has already given you everything you need. The answer to every desire you have and goal you are striving for is already within you. The only problem is that you are not enough to call it forth on your own power and strength. It can only be called forth in the name of Jesus. You have to fully get this in your spirit to be able to apply this work.

Once you remember that the Kingdom of God (not Heaven, these are two different places) is within you, then that leaves the question that you may be asking yourself, "If everything I need is within me, then how do I activate the power of God that is already within me so it can become manifest?" Read on and I will teach you how.

Activating the Kingdom of God

There are four steps to activating the manifestation of the power of God that lives within you. They are:

1. Decide

2. Believe

3. Speak/Command

4. Action

One morning as I was sitting during my prayer and meditation time, praying for my day and asking God what He would have me do for the day. I had already written out my Impossible list for the day (I go into this whole process on my CD,

The Realm of The Impossible: Walking With The God of Miracles) and I was on the item of getting more than 10 people registered for an upcoming workshop and it was the last day for Early Bird registration and it felt like I was far away from reaching my goal.

I then followed the teaching of Dr. David Yonggi Cho, the pastor of the largest church in the world, in his book, *The Fourth Dimension,* that shared that visioning is one of the languages of the Holy Spirit. I was seeing each of the items on my to-do list coming to pass in my mind's eye. Then, I heard the voice of God say, "But you haven't decided." Whoa! I just sat there for a moment to take in what I had just heard.

God was right. I had not decided. I was going through the motions of hoping, but I had not made a decision that it was *going* to happen today. I realized that I was still hoping and wishing that it would be done, but I was not in a space of certainty, which is what God requires of you and I before He moves.

I focused my mind, commanding my spirit to line up with the Word that says that anything is possible through Christ who strengthens me, and decided that it was done. I began speaking the Word that tells me that anything I ask in the name of Jesus will be done for me. I sat and spoke the Word of God until something shifted in place within me. I knew I had decided.

Once I decided, I then asked myself, "Do I really believe?" Yes, I did. I could feel that it was literally done. I realized that I was onto something. God was teaching me the steps to activating His indwelling spirit to manifest in my life. I knew that while deciding is the first step, it was not enough.

I knew that I also had to believe. It is a prerequisite to experiencing God. You must believe that He is a God that keep His promises and gives you what you ask in Jesus' name if you do not doubt (Mark 11:22). I knew I was in the space of believing when I could open and stretch my mind to seeing it as done. Yet, it still felt like there was another step.

Once I decided and believed, I then had to command and speak it. Once you decide and believe the evidence of your belief is that you move into action. Taking action and moving forward in faith then becomes easy. The level of action you take in alignment with God's Word is the measure of your faith. Faith is not waiting in stillness for God. It is continuing to serve God as you move forward on His Word. Faith is boldly moving forward. There is no such thing as faith without action. In your process of activating the Kingdom of God within you, the Holy Spirit is the key.

The level of action you take in alignment with God's Word is the measure of your faith.

Hearing from the Holy Spirit

One Sunday evening as I was juggling all I have to do in my ministry as the preacher, trainer, minister, janitor, administrative assistant, marketer and promoter, I missed the deadline to promote an upcoming workshop in a local natural health magazine, *Natural Awakenings.* I had already turned off my laptop and was heading up to bed for the night.

Just as my right foot landed on the first step to head upstairs, God nudged me and instructed me to look in the pile on the corner of my desk. I turned around and began thumbing through the pile. As soon as my hand landed on the Natural Awakenings, something deep within my spirit felt like it clicked. I knew that this was what God had me looking for.

I opened up the magazine and saw that the deadline for submitting calendar events for the next month had passed by one day. I thought, "Maybe they aren't working on the weekend and if I submit it tonight, they will still include it in the next issue." I was right.

The next morning my telephone rang and it was the magazine's editor in chief, Dee. The first thing she said to me after I answered was that she had been looking for a Christian who did this work. From that day forward, Dee and I formed an instant connection and she has whole-heartedly supported my work. That was more than a year ago.

As I was just beginning to share this deliverance work in a tele-conference, I was not aware that Dee was one of the callers on the line. It was a whole new level and realm of work for me and I kept saying, "You all must think I'm crazy and I've lost my mind" during the call.

Dee called in the next few days and we had a great discussion about the teachings I was sharing. She shared that the work was right on and that she could tell that people were so captivated during the call and that they knew in their spirits that it was not only the truth, but the insights they had been praying for.

Dee has a gift of being able to hear the Holy Spirit very clearly and concisely. As a matter of fact, God allowed her to have a non-stop ringing sound in her ear so she could get to a level of mastery in hearing His voice over anything else. One of the things Dee said during our conversation was that she hoped that I included a portion in my upcoming book (the one you are now holding in your hands!) that taught about the importance of being able to hear the Holy Spirit in this work. I replied, "Yes, like the Prego spaghetti commercial – it's in there." We both laughed.

I could not write a complete teaching on this work without including a section that deals with the critical importance of you being able to hear clearly from the Holy Spirit in order to move in deliverance. These teachings came directly from the Holy Spirit.

As I asked God questions, I would receive answers and then I would inquire about where the corresponding scripture was in the Bible. Without fail, He always guided me to it. The teaching came directly from God and then He always showed me the scripture in His word to confirm His instruction.

Prior to moving in this work, I thought that my primary gift was my ability to deliver transformative teaching as a speaker. Not so. One day last summer as I was standing in the shower, I was unabashedly seeking God on moving in the next realm of my gifting. As clearly as I heard each pellet of water stream from the shower head, I heard His voice say, "Speaking is not your primary gift."

"What!?? Then what is my primary gift?" I asked.

"Your one true gift is hearing my voice. I gave you the gift of speaking and teaching so you can tell others what you hear."

I was surprised by this. I asked, "But doesn't everyone have the ability to hear directly from you?"

"Everyone has a measure, but then there are those with an extra measure and not everyone has that. You are one of the rare people who have an extra measure."

It wasn't until a half a year later as I was doing a deliverance session over the phone with an incredible child of God, Claire, that I heard God share His name for my gift. Claire was sharing how she had prayed and asked God for the gift of "having a heart that perpetually hears from Heaven." He responded one day by telling her that He had granted her prayer and it is a rare gift that He rarely gives out and that He had given me the same gift. She was calling to tell me what He said to her.

Whether or not you are one of the rare children of God whom He has blessed with a heart that perpetually hears from Heaven, you must develop your ability to hear directly from God in order to move forward in His will for your life.

When I am doing the work of cleaning a heart and spirit, it is the Holy Spirit that literally shows me things from your past and allows me to feel what you feel. When I am doing a clearing of someone's heart, God has given me the ability to connect so deeply with you that I can literally see pieces of your life that God needs me to see from your childhood as if it were a slide show running on a blank, white wall in front of me.

I can immediately tell what someone needs or how they are feeling. And now I can feel which stronghold spirits you are dealing with and precisely how they manifest in your life. I still have a difficult time in large crowds because of the spiritual chatter of everyone's "stuff" can be quite distracting.

I have mastered being able to tune it out unless I am using the gifts to move in God's Kingdom. I think that is why I can be so focused now because I have had to learn how to have laser-beam focus on the task at-hand just so I don't feel like I am walking around overly sensitive and exposed.

When I am doing the work of cleaning hearts and spirits, the Holy Spirit also shows me images of how the unclean spirits are oriented and attached within a temple. God allows me to feel how the person I am working with feels. I know when we are in the process of "loosening up" an unclean spirit because I inevitably feel it within my own body. No matter what gifts you have, this is where the Holy Spirit needs you to be to move in deliverance.

There is a process that will strengthen your ability to hear directly from God. Jesus had to go to the Father so the Holy Spirit, the Comforter, the Spirit of Truth could come and take up residence inside of you. You are the representation of Jesus in the earth. This gives you the ability to be instructed by God in all you do. Hearing from the Holy Spirit requires time and is by far, your most precious resource.

✓

Creating a more intimate relationship with the Holy Spirit begins with focused intention and giving more time to God. I'm sure you have heard before that it works just like a relationship in the natural – it takes spending quality time together on a daily basis and God will open your ears so you can hear Him clearly.

Here are the steps to clearing the way: *Mornings*

1. Decide

2. Give God the first fruits of your time.

3. Begin by entering into His presence with scripture.

> Praying for supplications, worshipping God, making intercessions for others and giving God thanks are all part of the order of prayer that follows the reading of scripture (1 Timothy 2:1). Once each of these activities are done, but you must add something to your spiritual routine. You must ask Him questions, meditate, and sit still long enough to hear God respond to you.
>
> The key to this is sitting through two critical stages – what I call the task voice and "itchy-twitchies."

4. Sit still long enough to listen.

5. Renew Your Mind around His Word and what He is instructing you.

The Power of Belief

Let me share with you the story of how the Holy Spirit brought me the understanding of the power of belief. As I was lying in bed one morning last summer and asking God what He would have me focus on that day to move His vision forward. He replied, "Belief. You have to work on your belief."

Now, you have to understand that at the time, I had been doing full-time ministry for more than seven years and had been on this path for nineteen years. Everyday of the last seven years of my life has been on faith, and for God to say that I had to work on my belief was hard to hear. My ego was screaming, "What?! What do you mean work on my belief?!"

I caught myself before my ego got out of control and submitted to His words. I knew that there was a whole new place that God wanted to take me. I had to be a teachable and willing student. God is infinite and as soon as you think you really have something down, He will come along and blow it to pieces to teach you a whole new dimension in Him. This is a life-time work.

I asked him, "Where should I begin?" He flashed before my mind's eye the Excel spreadsheet I had just put together the day before of the financial forecast for the ministry. He said, "You wrote down the numbers but you do not believe me for them." I had to stop and admit that it was true.

My mind was not renewed around believing God for the forecasted finances of the ministry. It took me about a day to let this sink into my spirit – it was time to go to a new level of belief in God. The next level of teaching came the next day. God knew that I needed a day to move this teaching from the knowledge level to the understanding level. I said out loud, "Tell me more, Lord. Tell me more Holy Spirit. Teach me. I am ready to learn. Teach me. "

He began to show me that there is a level of reality for which I did not believe Him. As my eyes were closed, He showed me the top of my head with a large, rubber band-like circle coming out from it. I knew that this circle represented my mind. Inside the circle were the images of my current belief. I was ashamed to see how little was inside of the circle. That day my rent was not even inside of the circle.

Believing God

Outside of the circle were the images I had posted on my vision board. I saw everything from the arena full of people I will be preaching to one day to the IPod speaker system I desired outside of the circle. I was blown away to be shown a snapshot of my current belief. I *wanted* to believe God for the things outside of the circle but the truth was, I did not. I was not there yet. I had to stretch and wrap my mind around the very things I envisioned.

When I was at my Sunday training class at Zion Christian Training Center last week, in the midst of Apostle's deep teaching on becoming the true offspring of God, he said, "There is only one little word that is holding back the Body of Christ – unbelief." It is so true. The Body of Christ is stuck in a crisis of unbelief and it is causing us to miss God. You cannot move into faith until you first believe.

Before you go any further, stop and take a look at your current level of belief. When I say belief, be very clear that I do not mean hoping or wanting. They exist on the way to belief, but they are not belief.

Belief is being absolutely certain of something whether or not it can be seen with your natural eyes. Once you believe something, you will naturally take action on your belief. While believing opens the door, it will not get you there until you take action. Taking action on those things that are yet unseen is faith. Faith provides the seed of what God needs to manifest in your life. Without belief you will never have faith.

You know what the Word says, but what do you *really* believe?

- Do you believe God for your healing or do you think that sickness is just something you have to exist with?

- Do you believe God for that financial freedom or do you believe financial struggle is something you have to live with as a believer?

- Do you believe that being someone who has dedicated their life to Christ means struggle and strife?

- Do you believe that dedicating your life to Christ means living your life more abundantly?

- Do you believe that you have the power, dominion, authority to cast devils out of people, be in the midst of darkness and not be overtaken, and lay hands on the sick and they will be healed? (Mark 16:17)

You always get what you believe.

You always get what you believe. You can always tell what you believe by taking an objective look at your life. Your current life is an amalgamation of your beliefs. Whatever you have believed up to this point in your life has manifested – nothing more; nothing less.

Your mind is the gateway to your belief and belief is the gateway to your blessings. Before you move on, stop, and take a good, honest look at the level of belief that you move in. Perhaps you are stuck and not growing in your faith because you don't believe God for the very things you are asking of Him. In order to believe, you have to have a renewed mind.

Renewing Your Mind

The easiest way for me to share with you the process of renewing your mind is to share a response that I replied to an e-community member of mine. She emailed an *"Ask Ericka"* question asking me if there was a certain process for renewing her mind. I get this question often and I would like to share my response to Nikki with you.

Nikki, yes, sound of his voice, the core process is similar for all of us. You will want to set aside time in the morning before you begin your day.

Find a special place for you - a chair, pillow, etc. Something other than the bed that is still in your bedroom and not the main part of the house as it provides too many distractions. I use a set of large pillows that I just keep on the floor in my bedroom.

I actually begin by writing out the scripture from the most recent sermon or Bible study I have attended in a notebook I keep for all of my sermon notes. This helps me get into the Word and make a transition.

I remain in the Word until I feel that "relief" that only the Word of God can provide. Once I have been in the Word, I then begin to renew my mind. I check in with my mind by asking the following questions: 1) Mind, how are you doing today? 2) What do I believe God for right now? 3) What am I willing to believe God for?

Then, I begin the process of praying. I begin my prayer by thanking God. I transition my prayer to confession and asking God for what I need and for the needs of others.

Once I am done praying, I sit still and focus on "stretching my mind" around what it is I am asking from God. In other words, I practice believing God for the things I have prayed for and have on my "to do" list and the things that are needed and desired for my vision to move forward.

I then spend as much time as I can just sitting there. If I have any questions to ask the Holy Spirit, I ask. If not, I just sit and ask God what He would have me work on today and to whom He would have me minister.

The key is to make the time to sit there until you get through the chattering voices in your head. I call this my "task voice." Once you begin to allow those voices to chatter (the ones that will talk about your To Do List for the day, etc.) your body will begin to get uncomfortable. Your toe might itch, your back might bother you. Sit still through those distractions from your flesh (I call these the itchy-twitchies).

On the other side of the distractions is the silence of the Holy Spirit - God's voice. It's unmistakable. You will know when you hear it.

Your process may be different from mine, but the point is to begin to find your process. However you need to get into your still space, allow it to unfold.

You will always want to be in the Word before you pray and pray before you meditate. The prayer is you speaking to God and meditation is God speaking back to you. The time may vary in how long it takes to get to the voice of the Holy Spirit, but it is there, waiting for you to find it. It may even take several days of walking through the steps, but it is there just waiting for you. I hope that helps...Love, Ericka

The key is that you create the time in your daily routine (that is a book in and of itself) to ask and listen for answers from The Holy Spirit. I do this directly following my prayer time by moving into a quiet space of meditation (listening for God's direction and insight). If I don't clearly and concisely hear from God during my meditation time or if another question comes up that I need an answer to, I literally put myself on a talk fast or refrain from talking as long as possible until the answer I need comes. The key is that the Holy Spirit shows up its strongest in silence.

Step Into All Jesus Has For You

Jesus is part divine and part human in nature. You may know the human aspect of the man named Jesus well and his teachings in the Bible. Yet, God is requiring of you to learn even more about the heavenly aspect of who Jesus is and what it affords you as a believer.

You can call on the name of Jesus and it causes everything to line up and come into submission to the power of your words (you must speak it out loud). Every circumstance, person, thought, blessing, vision, action and manifestation must come into alignment with who Jesus says you are and the power that has been granted to you. You can literally speak forth things that are not yet manifested into existence. This is how powerful you are.

You can literally speak forth things that are not yet manifested into existence. This is how powerful you are.

A great way to examine the amount of power currently in your life is to ask yourself whether or not every area of your life is a reflection of the glory of God. Through Jesus, you have the power to cause every aspect of your life to line up with who He says you are and what He says you have. When The Holy Spirit lives within you, you automatically long to line up with who God says you are.

I always love uncovering opportunities for improvement in my life. Making the necessary changes and adjustments certainly keeps me busy and focused forward. I invite you to do the same.

79

Take a good, objective look around your life right now. Ask yourself the following questions:

What areas are in alignment with who you know yourself to be in Jesus?

_____

_____

_____

_____

_____

_____

What areas are not in alignment with the power and presence of Jesus in your life?

_____

_____

_____

_____

_____

_____

Now that you have reminded yourself of where you are this very moment, you can begin to step into all you are in Jesus. During coaching sessions when clients are working to move from a limited space in their lives to becoming who they know they can be, they discover that there is a gap in their belief that they must work on closing in order to move them forward. Taking a closer look at your belief is necessary before you can move on.

The God of the Impossible

Several months later God brought another level to this teaching. He told me one morning as I was renewing my mind, "It's time to believe me for the impossible." Whoa! He then said, "Impossible is not what you think it is. When I had the scriptures written, what I meant by impossible is different from what you think it is."

Of course, I was sitting there saying, "Okay, Lord, tell me more." He continued, "You think impossible means that it can't be done. You think impossible means a dreamland fantasy like dreaming the 'impossible' dream (Just then, He put the melody to the song, *To Dream the Impossible Dream* in my head). That is not what I meant when I had that scripture written." He then dropped the doozey on me and said, "Impossible is actually the area just outside of your belief. That is where I dwell."

Impossible is actually the area just outside of your belief.

He continued, "Your impossible changes everyday." I was so glad I was sitting down because those words blew me away. Did you know that your impossible changes everyday? Let me prove it to you.

Depending on how renewed your mind is, you can wake up on a Monday morning and feel like you can do anything. You can take a look at an item on your 'to-do' list and say, "I can do this!" Yet, there are still things on that list just outside of what you feel capable of doing or know how to do – that is *your* impossible.

One day your impossible may be getting through all of the items on your 'to-do' list and still getting to bed on time. Yet, you cannot see your way through it, it feels impossible to you. Then, the next day your impossible may be getting through a large presentation or getting the capitalization that your ministry or business needs to move forward. Perhaps it feels impossible for your ministry to fully financially support you and your family.

As the Holy Spirit was "downloading" this into me, He began to show me some of my "impossibles." While I had listed them as goals, once I began to understand what the Holy Spirit was telling me, I understood that those goals still felt impossible for me. He then brought to my remembrance the scripture Matthew 19:26, *"And Jesus looked at them and said, 'With men this is impossible but with God all things are possible.'"*

He continued to share that my impossible is different from someone else's impossible. I could literally feel the shackles of limitation coming off of my mind. I began to internalize for the first time in my life that God is a God of the impossible.

He began to breath into me that if there was a realm called, "impossible," than the opposite exists. I began to understand that there are two different realms, one called 'the possible' and one called 'the impossible'. It is up to you to determine which realm you live in.

It took about a day for my spirit to fully absorb these new teachings. I then cleared out an entire day just for God and asked Him, "God what would you have me do today?" I ended up driving by a bookstore here in Raleigh called *Stevens Bookstore*, which is an incredible theological bookstore to which my friend, Dee, introduced me. It is a bookstore with half of a million books in this huge warehouse (with no air conditioning, I might add). God sent me there that day, but I did not know what I was looking for.

I began walking up and down the many aisles full of boxes and piles of books. I knew that God sent me there for a specific purpose. There were boxes with books on top of the boxes in every aisle of the store. I truly needed God's guidance on what He had me there to find.

I remember thinking, "Father God, where would you have me begin?" He asked me, "What do you want to learn?" I told Him that I wanted to learn about Him as the God of the impossible. I wondered if anyone had done a study and written about Him being the God of the impossible. I began to browse the shelves and look for books with the Word 'impossible' in the title. I was actually dumb-founded at just how few there were.

As I was standing there with my purse over my shoulder, I asked the Holy Spirit to show me what He wanted me to have. Then, something happened that surprised me.

With no contact whatsoever, a pile of books fell over behind me. I didn't even tap the pile with my hip or purse yet six or seven books just fell off of the top of the pile onto the floor (and I might add that they moved with some force behind them). I stood there looking down both sides of the aisle thinking, "Now, I know I did not touch these books." I knew that God was trying to tell me something.

I looked down at the book that had been uncovered when the others fell over. There was an old, tattered book entitled, *The War on The Saints*. The top page of the book was a dingy shade of cream and did not even have a cover with the name of its author.

The Holy Spirit said, "Get that book." He had already prompted me to pick up another book and I asked, "Can I go now?" He replied, "You can go to check out." As I was standing at the gray laminate check out counter, I spotted another book on the hold shelf behind the cash register. I knew in my spirit that this was the book that God intended me to purchase. It was another book on spiritual warfare. I knew I had everything I needed and checked out. When I got home, I sat my pile of books in the chair near my front door and headed out that evening.

The next day I got to the first book in my pile, it was the tattered and worn book. I opened the book and my eyes immediately read the words, "Satan's Ground." I knew God was doing something that moment. I asked Him, "What does that mean? What is Satan's ground?"

He brought the teachings of the realm of the impossible and the possible to my remembrance. He continued to tell me that Satan's ground, then, is the realm of the possible. God gave Satan authority over the realm of the possible. Stay with me on this one...I need you to get this.

I knew then that if there was such a thing as Satan's ground, then there had to be the opposite -or "non-Satan's" ground. I allowed this new revelation to seep into my spirit and continued to inquire for more. I said to myself, "Wait a minute – if there is Satan's ground, then there has got to be Holy ground. There's got to be a place that Satan does not have access."

He told me that there is a realm to which Satan has no access. He told me that it is what I had been calling, the realm of the impossible. The realm of the impossible is where God functions. Satan has no jurisdiction in the realm of the impossible.

If God created all things, then He allows the presence of Satan. That means that He must have created boundaries or territory for Satan. That led me to understand that there exists a space in which you can live where Satan cannot touch you – Holy Ground. I was hungry for more.

There is a realm in which you can live where Satan cannot touch you.

You Are Holy Ground

My next question to God was, "How do I know what is possible ground or Satan's ground and how to I know what is impossible ground or Holy ground?"

God shared with me how to you know when you are walking in the realm of the possible. The realm of the possible is where ego or self lives. When you are in the realm of possible, you say things like "I, my, mine..." *My* business. *My* ministry. *My* husband. *My* church. *My* pastor. *My* car. *My* house. *My* money. Anytime you allow ego into it, you will experience opposition, challenges and hindrances because Satan operates through your ego, flesh, and the things of this world.

The evidence that you are operating in the realm of the possible in any area of your life is lack, strife, stress, struggle, or challenges that seem beyond the norm. When you act as though that possession, position, church, job, or relationship is yours, you have to figure everything out with your own mind. It means that it is not fully dedicated to God and is still open to attack from the enemy.

When you think you can do it, you are in the realm of possible. You think it is about your know-how and that your hard work will get your through. No, no, no. The Truth is that you can do little to nothing operating in your own power

When you dedicated your life to the Lord, your life and everything in it became God's. You began the process of dying to self. Nothing belongs to you anymore. You have nothing. You are nothing without Christ.

You know you are in the realm of possible when God blesses you with an idea and you say, "Thank you for blessing me with this idea God. Now I know what to do and I can make it happen." And you try to take it from there. Without fail you begin to experience lack, strife, struggle, back-biting and suffering.

All too often believers witness this dynamic in the area of money and finances because too many of us believe that the money is ours. That is why it can be so difficult to let go of our money in tithes and offerings. We have a hard time letting it go and believing God is going to multiply it. It is not yours, it is only on loan. God blessed you with every penny in your wallet right now, every picture on your wall, every toe on your foot, every child that you have, every client, every car, everything you have. Everything you have belongs to God.

As long as you have neglected to dedicate it as Holy Ground, you are walking in the realm of possible where Satan and his evil and unclean spirits have access to your life, even as a believer. The problem is that you may not have dedicated is as Holy Ground – or that which belongs entirely to God.

While I was clear that blessings came from God, I was thinking and acting as though once God blessed me with something, it was mine to take from there. I thought that is what managing the things of God meant. Not so. When God brought that revelation to me, I felt like the wind had been knocked out of me.

I immediately began confessing, "Lord God, I confess that I thought this was mine. I thought you gave these gifts, talents, blessings and things to me. I thought this was *my* money and *my* ministry."

The next question I then asked was, "God, then how do I move something from Satan's ground (the realm of possible) to Holy Ground (the realm of the impossible)?" He showed me the image of a family bringing their child to the Lord for a christening or a baby dedication at a church.

That father and mother hold that baby up to God and say, "God we give this child to you. We know that you have blessed us with its care, but we know that this child belongs to you. We call forth a hedge of protection and abundance on this life. We dedicate our child to you." That child becomes Holy Ground.

Take a look at every area of your life, especially where there is strife, struggle, anxiety, worry, doubt, sickness, lack, or anything that is not of God. Any of those things that are not from God are of Satan, and they can only exist on Satan's ground. You must go through dedicating every belonging and every aspect of your life back to God and declaring it as Holy Ground. I included the prayer God spoke through me that day at the end of this chapter so you can go through your own Holy Ground dedication.

Developing Your Impossible Faith

Do you know how powerful you are? You have the authority to speak to anything and any spirit and it must obey. Walking in this space of who you really are means living in the realm of the impossible. You serve a God of miracles, signs and wonders just as powerful today as they were when the scriptures were written. Actually, Jesus himself said that you should do greater things than even He did (John 5:20).

How do you begin to tap into God of the impossible and leave behind any experience of God as a just-getting-by God? To serve a God of the impossible, you have to first understand the three levels of education in God and let it take root in your spirit and life.

There are three levels of education that the Holy Spirit shared with me. They are levels of knowledge, understanding, and evidence.

The Knowledge Level. You are at this level when you know, remember, and have memorized certain scriptures. At this first level – the knowledge level – another person can teach you. You can be sitting under a pastor, apostle, take a class, read a book or self-study, listen to sermons, and attend conferences to accumulate more knowledge and information. This is the level a majority of the Body of Christ is living in right now. God has two more levels that He requires of you.

The Understanding Level. The second level of education is called *understanding*. Understanding is the level where your knowledge begins to get inside of your spirit and the Word takes root in your heart. You no longer have to rely on your mind to remember what the scripture says because it now lives in your heart.

You can know something at the understanding level of education and still not understand it in your spirit. This level ushers you from your old self to your new self. This is where you become anew. The old things are passing away and you are becoming a new creature. Your cravings and desires change. The people you hang around change. The things you are willing to accept and the way you allow people to speak to you changes and you deeply desire the things of Jesus.

You know someone is at the level of understanding when you look at them and think, "Brother Jimmy is different. He is not the same person that I knew three years ago." You know it by the way he walks, talks, and his very presence because he is now walking in Christ and no longer in the world. That is how you know you have moved into the level of understanding in your Godly education. Once you move to understanding, there is a whole new level that God desires to take you to and from which you have to learn to live your life. It is the level of evidence.

The Evidence Level. When you begin to study and learn in a particular area of learning, until you demonstrate your effectiveness in that area, you are not fully educated. You have not fully manifested anything. You are not doing anything with your understanding yet.

Until you begin to demonstrate evidence of the presence of the Holy Spirit in all walks of your life, you are not fully educated in the things of God. It doesn't matter how much scripture you have memorized. The only thing that matters is how much scripture you are manifesting.

You are in the evidence level when someone looks at your life, they know that you are an ambassador for Jesus. They will want to meet your God because of the amazing results or fruit you produce in the realm of the impossible. In order to move from understanding to evidence, you must practice it as a part of your daily life.

How do you begin to practice moving in the realm of impossible? By commanding your mind, body and spirit to line up with the Word of God, then applying the power of God that you have in your tongue to speak things from nothingness into existence.

Devin, a brother of mine in Christ, captured it well when he once said to me, "You know it is God's vision when it seems so big that you cannot hold it in your hands and you say, 'God, are you sure you chose me for this?' You know because it is so big that only God can do it." If you could do it yourself, it would have been done. If it was possible you would not need God. When something is possible, you don't need God. That is why God is the God of the impossible

---

When something is possible, you don't need God.

Defining Your Impossible

In order for God to do the impossible for you, you must be very clear about what impossible looks like. Remember, your impossible is just outside of what you believe God for today – right now.

Maybe right now your impossible is having the resources you need today to pay your bills. Here is the catcher – the Holy Spirit instructed me that I was to write down what my impossible was every single day. Once I wrote it down, I was to stretch my mind to believe it and go to the scripture, Luke 18:27, "But he said the things that which are impossible with men are possible with God," and Luke 1:37, where it says, "For with God nothing will be impossible."

You must understand how to open up the impossible to your belief system. You may have been calling on a prince of the possible or of the world, which is Satan. Jesus requires you to persist until you learn this. He "sits" back and observes until you realize that it is impossible for you. Command the daily presence of God to do the impossible in your life.

You must declare it out loud:

pray for the impossible

"*Father God, in the name of Jesus, I believe you for the impossible today. Your Word says that with you, nothing is impossible. God, I call on you to do the impossible for me today so I can further your vision and touch the lives you have ordained me to touch. This is what your Word says that you will do. I believe in signs and wonders and stand on your Word. Lord, I ask you to do the impossible today. This is what impossible looks like for me today:" [list the specifics of your impossible for the day.]*

Do you know what you call it when God moves in the realm of the impossible? A miracle, sign or wonder. Are you ready for a life that is full of signs and wonders every day? Are you expecting God to show up mightily today? Right now? You serve a God of right now, so you have to stay in the present. God is a right now God.

Are you ready for a life that is full of signs and wonders every day?

That is where God wants to take you. Your signs and wonders will be different than mine because your impossible is different than my impossible. What does your impossible look like today?

- Does your impossible look like getting three more sales for your business?

- Does your impossible look like truly staying present and having a peaceful day today?

- Does your impossible look like having more than enough financially?

- Does your impossible look like your spouse demonstrating his or her love for you in the way you need to see it?

- Does your impossible look like eating right for the temple God lent you as a body? What does your impossible look like today?

Here is the key – you have to write it down.

You have to write it down.

Everyday. I have a catch-all notebook in which I keep everything, from grocery lists, to messages, to my 'to-do' lists. I keep it with me at all times so I always have what I need. This is where I keep my daily impossible list. He has done multiple signs and wonders since He showed me this revelation and process.

- Are you willing to believe God to show up as a God of the impossible for you?

- Will you allow God to be God?

- Will you allow Him to do what He does? He does the impossible, period. If it is less than impossible, He does not show up.

Will you allow Him to do what He does? He does the impossible, period. If it is less than impossible, He does not show up.

Until the day God uncovered this teaching, I believed that impossible meant that something could not be done. The Greek word for impossible is "adunatĕō," it says "not to have strength, power or ability, to be weak; or cannot be done." Until today, perhaps that is what you believed.

Impossible actually means just the opposite. It means that it can be done with God. What is impossible with man is possible with God. For with God nothing will be impossible.

Here is the amazing thing about walking this process out. Once you make your list of your daily impossible, you don't even have to believe God for the individual things. I lay hands on my impossible list and say:

> "Father, this feels impossible for me today and I know this is where you move and what you do. Father, in the name of Jesus, I stand on your Word and I line my mind up with the truth that tells me with man it is impossible but with God all things are possible. Lord, today I know for you this list is possible. God, do what you do. Father, in the name of Jesus, bring these things forth today in the name of Jesus."

You will begin to experience mighty and amazing signs and wonders when you incorporate this process into your life. It requires going through the specific process of being ushered into the realm of the impossible daily.

Holy Ground
A PRAYER FOR YOU

Here is a prayer that I said in my process of rededicating every aspect of my life to God as Holy Ground. I'll use a prayer to rededicate your finances to God as an example, but you should go through every area of your life and do this same process, no matter what it is.

Father, in the name of Jesus, I just confess in the name of Jesus and ask your forgiveness because I thought this area of my life was mine. I thought the money (or fill in whatever you are dedicating) was mine, Lord. I knew that it was from you, but I forgot that it is yours and that I am just the administrator. So, Lord God, I humbly ask your forgiveness today and I confess that I was wrong. Today, I repent and I renounce those thoughts and behaviors.

Lord, I thank you for every penny and every ounce of prosperity, every dollar and every bit of wealth, health, joy and life that I experience. I know it all comes from you, God, but I forgot that it is yours. Today, Lord, I dedicate my finances and every aspect of my life back to you. I dedicate them to you as Holy Ground.

In the name of Jesus, Satan, you no longer have jurisdiction or access to these finances because they are 100% God's. They belong to God. They are Holy Ground. Right now, in the name of Jesus, anything that is not in the image and likeness of God is commanded to leave right now. Spirit of Bondage that has manifested in poverty, you are cast out right now in Jesus' name. Lack, you are cast out in the name of Jesus. Struggle, you are now cast out in the name of Jesus. You are to never return to my life or anyone in my life in any way, form or fashion in the name of Jesus.

Father God, in the name of Jesus, from this day forward, I leave behind the realm of possible and now walk in the realm of the impossible with all of your might, power, glory and magnificence.

I honor you with the finances that you have blessed me with. I will be most careful to ask you how you would have me spend your money. And, Lord God, most of all, I promise to humbly and gratefully, and most carefully give you all the praise and all the glory. I know, Lord, that it is not mine, it is yours. All this I ask in Jesus' name. Amen.

Go through every area of your life and speak this prayer over it. And I do mean everything, from your wardrobe to your child. Your car and anything else in your body or that comes in contact with your body as you move through your day. Remember to dedicate your mind, ideas, thoughts, friends, business or ministry, church, blankets, furnishings, dishes, office supplies, computer – I mean everything and anything you use to live from and touch the lives of others with – to God.

Chapter Five

Your Fearless Foundation

Now that you are armed with the process to enter into the realm of the impossible, we have to address the biggest issue holding the Body of Christ captive – fear. It is possible to be filled with the Holy Spirit, praise and worship, know the Word and still be in fear about walking out God's purpose and calling for your life. It is time to deal with the issue of fear once and for all. It is my charge in this chapter to guide you into a space where you not only imagine your life without fear, but actually live it.

There are institutes, classes, workshops, and books solely dedicated to the topic of fear. Once you understand the truth about fear, you can get on with the business of bringing forth the incredible vision that God has planted in you.

To move forward, you must also understand what fear is not - it is *not* False Evidence Appearing Real. This is the definition of fear I have seen over and over again and it is not fully accurate. I felt like I would scream if I saw this definition in another book or heard another speaker refer to it.

The truth is that we have to stop perpetuating this lie about fear because it keeps us operating out of our egos and not our spirits – where fear exists.

You must understand the spiritual nature of fear and use tools from God to guide your way through fear. Fear is not something just in your mind. Fear is not just doubt or your negative thoughts. Fear is a spiritual issue and simply cannot be reckoned with in your mind, your will, or your ego.

You may have been taught that fear is your enemy and that you can fight it. You may have believed until now that you can affirm or attempt to overcome your fear with positive self-talk and cute affirmations posted on your bathroom mirror. You cannot ever affirm your way out of fear. Affirmations will help for a minute, but your fear will come up again shortly and take hold of you.

Perhaps you have been trying to push or move forward in spite of your fear. Fear is the way you can monitor the spiritual doors through which darkness enters your thoughts, habits, and life. Fear illuminates the areas of your life in which you do not believe God will provide for you.

My work with fearlessness began years ago after hundreds of client coaching sessions. A clear pattern emerged of the three things that were stopping believers from moving forward in their vision – fear, lack of dominion and authority, and lack of structured time to manifest His vision. The most prevalent of these three hindrances was fear.

God designed you to be fearless and gave you an unstoppable spirit. Yet, His children are being too easily deterred and falling out of the race to receive His rewards. Once God shared with me what fear really was about, these teachings revolutionized the lives of all who learned them.

Everyone I came in contact with, who so deeply desired to live out the fullness of obedience to God in their lives and professed to love Him with all of their hearts, souls, and minds, was dealing with fear. Their fear was stopping them from being obedient to God, no matter how bad they wanted to.

The old motivational-era's definition of fear – feel it and do it anyway – was not working. Fear had managed to paralyze the lives of God's children. I asked God why He allowed it if He knew that it was fear that was the main culprit in stopping the Body from moving His work forward in the world.

The Two Types of Fear

There are two distinctly different types of fear in the Word. It is easy to get these two types of fear mixed up using the English translation of the Word. You must look back into Greek to understand the distinction of these two types of fear.

The first type of fear is used in context as "The fear of the Lord." The Greek word for this type of fear is *eulabeia*, which refers to the reverence, awe and honor of God, for example, in Psalm 2:11 (*"Serve the Lord with fear and rejoice with trembling"*) and Proverbs 9:10 (*"The fear of the Lord is the beginning of wisdom..."*). This is not referring to the spirit of fear.

The fear that the spirit of fear refers to is the Greek word *deilas*, which refers to fright or dread. Even as I write these words, I am laughing to myself to see just how much I have come to know about fear and our relationship to it. I now see that it was just a stepping stone to where God was taking me.

The Truth About Fear

Eight years ago, I walked away from my stifling corporate job as an Administrative Recruiter (I think they gave me some fancy title, but that was the gist of it) to honor my deep desire knowing that it was time to live God's purpose full-time. As I looked around at the five-hundred square-foot, one bedroom apartment my seven year old daughter and I had lived in for more than a year to minimize expenses. I just knew I *had* to "get" this in order to move out of this miniscule apartment. I was at the end of what I knew to do.

The next voice I heard was not my own. This voice came from within my spirit and said, "I have put all of the answers within my children and they are not being obedient. Your job is to help them be obedient to my call. If they will heed my call, the world will be transformed." I then saw images of famine, starving children, homelessness, poverty, and inner city crime flash through my mind.

Then the voice of God continued by saying, "I have put the answers to all of the world's problems in my children, if only they will be obedient. Your job is to help my children be obedient." From that day on, my fear disappeared and I deeply and profoundly understood my specific calling and purpose in this world. I have been heeding God's call to be a catalyst to guide God's children in full obedience with His call on their lives ever since.

About a year later, I was planning the lesson for the Teen Sunday School class I had taught for years at First AME Church in Seattle, Washington. I was preparing a lesson on fear, and as I was reading the Word about fear I noticed it was used in several different contexts. I needed a deeper understanding to be able to teach my students. I then asked the Lord, "I have read your Word and I am not clear about fear. Please reveal to me the truth about fear." In just moments, my reply came and said, "Fear is the lack of surrender or submission to God."

Wow! What!? I applied that definition and re-read the passages in the Word about fear and it fit! That was it! *Fear is the lack of surrender or submission to God.* I have been teaching it ever since and it has fit for everyone I have shared it with. Did you get it? *This* is the truth about fear. It is so important that you understand this; it is the cornerstone of this course. Here it is again...

Fear is the lack of surrender or submission to God.

Why God Allows Fear

Once I began moving in God's deeper revelation of fear, I inevitably had to just stop one day and ask God why He allows fear. I was wondering why the Sovereign, Almighty God who could easily just wipe fear and any unclean thing from our lives actually allows fear to exist and persist in our lives.

After I recorded my first CD on fear, *Freedom From Fear*, and wrote my first book on fear, *The Fearless Living Challenge*, God continued to pour more and more understanding about fear into me. I needed to know why God allowed fear. I was intrigued with the fact that He is such a mighty God and can literally do what we cannot in an instant. I found it odd that he allowed so much fear to overwhelm His believers.

That became a question I took directly to God for an answer. It wasn't long before He responded. He allows fear so you can identify the areas of your walk with God in which you do not believe the very things you are praying for. If you did not have fear, you would not be able to identify the areas that you have not surrendered or submitted to God.

If fear is "the lack of surrender or submission to God," then that means that fear is allowed so it can illuminate the areas of your life in which you are not believing God.

---

*Fear is allowed so it can illuminate the areas of
your life in which you are not believing God.*

In other words, by paying attention to your fear, you can identify the areas in which your faith is waning.

I also knew from 2 Timothy 1:7 that the spirit of fear is not from God. Yet nothing manifests in the natural without God allowing it. In other words, fear is not sent from God, but it is God allowed. That distinction led me to understand that it must be paramount to be clear about the areas of your life in which fear is showing up.

This becomes very important prior to actually casting fear out of your life because you need to understand what God is trying to show you through your fear. You will need to take some time to identify the areas that fear is showing up in your life. These areas literally provide a road-map to God for you and will illuminate your way out of fear and into faith.

No matter how tempting it may be to cast out your fear before you have taken the time to uncover the areas in which your faith is weak, do not proceed without this clarity. It is critical that you understand this before you go on to identifying any other unclean fruit that has found it's way into your life.

I already shared part of His response in that He allows fear because it illuminates the areas in which we do not believe Him. Any area in which you are experiencing fear is a lack of belief, and therefore, not faith.

---

*Any area in which you are experiencing fear is a
lack of belief, and therefore, not faith.*

He continued to respond in a way that was so clear, concise and made perfect sense. He told me that He allows fear because He requires of those who love Him to knock, seek and ask Him of the deeper things and mysteries of God so we step into our authority and dominion over fear and anything else that He allows in our lives. He requires us to overcome and persist and one of the things that you must overcome is fear.

It is important to know that casting out the spirit of fear does not remove your "flight or fight" response; you will still have your innate reaction to physical pain and that natural alarm or surprise reaction that keeps you safe in times when abrupt action is necessary for safety and survival.

From Fear to Faith

When you rid fear from your life, you begin to truly and deeply believe God for his promises. You then begin to take unstoppable action toward those things that He has called you to in faith. Once you are in faith, the doors open to walk into understanding the other thirteen stronghold spirits and how they show up in your life.

Once you have dealt with your fear, there is nothing that can hold you back from experiencing the life God created for you. You become the person God created you to be with no fear, emotional baggage or unclean spirits.

> *Fear illuminates the areas of your life in which*
> *you do not believe God will provide for you.*

The opposite of fear is faith. Fear and faith cannot co-exist. You have to choose one or the other. Once you believe God for that particular thing you feared before, it no longer has a stronghold on you and the spirit of fear will find somewhere else to reside. Removing fear from your life is the doorway to your will and God's will for you becoming one.

Now that you are clear about the true meaning and purpose of fear, it's time to take a good look at your life and identify the type of fear(s) you are facing. You may think of fear as one big insurmountable mountain yet haven't taken much time to see what the mountain is made of. Without knowing what your mountain of fear is comprised of, you will not be able to dismantle your fear very easily.

Let's take a look at the main types of fear. As you read these, make note of which ones are real for you right now. The main types of fear are:

1. Fear of failure
2. Fear of success
3. Fear of being alone
4. Fear of disappointment
5. Fear of rejection or of being hurt
6. Fear of not being or feeling loved
7. Fear of loss of privacy or the "fishbowl"
8. Fear of increased responsibility
9. Fear of being exposed

10. Fear of not having enough

11. Fear of abandonment

12. Physical fears or phobias (spiders, snakes, etc.)

How To Surrender Your Fear

Surrendering your fear means to relinquish or hand it over to God. Once you are aware of why it has been in your life, then you must let it go and give it to God.

Fear is a guide to illuminate those things and areas of your life that you have not yet surrendered to God.

The process of fully surrendering your fear is:

1. Confess your fears.

   The first step to moving beyond fear is to admit that you have been experiencing fear. You have to first identify the fears in your life in order to shine the light on them and pull them up by the root for good.

2. Remember what God has promised you.

   God has promised you great rewards as a believer. This step reminds you to reconnect with God's promises for your life. What visions have God shown you is possible for you? What has He promised you?

3. Identify what you are not believing God for.

To complete this step, you have to think about the goals that you have been writing down and your prayers. Have you been asking Him to send the right man for you,? Yet when you really take an honest look at it, you really don't believe that such a man exists or that you are worthy of that level of love? This step requires that you take a look at the things you have asked God for but have not really believed are attainable.

4. Imagine what it would be like without the fear.

As I stated at the beginning of this chapter, it is time to move beyond imagining life with no fear and actually live it. It actually disappears and you have to get your mind ready for its disappearance because you may have come to believe that fear is just part of the human experience. No, it is not. Imagine that fear in no longer an issue that slows you down or stops you from doing a single thing in your life. What would your life be like?

5. Pray the Prayer of Surrender.

As I learned to move through fear, I used to say a prayer about surrendering my fear each and every day. I share a prayer that you can use at the end of the chapter.

6. Cast out the spirit of fear.

I will share this process in detail in Chapter Nine: *Casting Out The Unclean*.

More on Fear

Intimately understanding fear was one of my Kingdom assignments and I have spent years studying its every dimension. This study resulted in my third book, *The Fearless Living*

Challenge: A 49-Day Course to Living Your Greatness. In this book, I actually walk you through the full process to creating a fearless life. It is available at www.erickajackson.com or at www.amazon.com. This book is for you if you want to give your life a fearless makeover.

For an in-depth understanding of fear as a stronghold spirit, see the section on The Spirit of Fear later in the book.

Activating God's Favor

Favor is really the next level beyond fear. Surrendering the fear ushers you into a realm few ever experience in life – the realm of walking in your God-given favor. Now that you know the steps to take to surrender your fear, we have to talk about understanding and activating God's favor in your life.

Favor is the state of being a reflection of God, where people recognize God within you and respond to you as a child of God. Favor goes beyond money and financial blessings. When you are walking in God's favor you receive supernatural treatment without even asking for it.

Being a child of God entitles you to experience God's favor and covering. This favor and covering provides you with some important benefits that non-believers do not have access to. This favor does not come from you and it is not for you. It comes from God and it is for His glory. This favor is activated once the Holy Spirit takes up residence in your temple by being born again.

One day at my church, I noticed a piece of goldenrod paper with some words typed on it stapled to a plain cork bulletin board in the foyer. I stopped and actually took a closer look at those words. I was blown away at the power of what they said. It was entitled, *Favor Confession*. It had no author or dates on it. I stood there and read the Words and my mouth dropped at their power, authority and expectation.

I am intentionally putting this confession on a page of its own so you can print it up and post it in a place that will remind you to walk in God's glory each and every day. Recite it every morning during your prayer and meditation time. Enjoy!

Favor Confession

Father, in the name of Jesus, I thank you for making me righteous and accepted through the blood of Jesus. Because of that, I am blessed and highly favored by you. I am the object of your affection. Your favor surrounds me as a shield and the first thing that people come into contact with is my favor shield.

Thank you that I have favor with you and man today. All day long, people go out of their way to bless and to help me. I will have favor with everyone that I deal with today. Doors that were once closed are now opened for me. I receive preferential treatment and I have special privileges. I am God's favored child.

No good thing will He withhold from me. Because of God's favor, my enemies cannot triumph over me. I have supernatural increase and promotion. I declare restoration of everything that the devil has stolen from me. I have honor in the midst of my adversaries and an increase of assets – especially in real estate and an expansion of territory.

Because I am highly favored by God, I experience great victories, supernatural turn-rounds and supernatural breakthroughs in the midst of great impossibilities. You receive recognition, prominence, and honor through me. Even ungodly authorities grant petitions to me. Policies, rules, regulations, and laws are changed and reversed on my behalf.

Battles ae won that I don't even have to fight because God fights them for me. This is the day, the set time and the designated moment for me to experience the free favors of God that profusely and lavishly abound on my behalf. - In Jesus' Name, Amen.

Isn't that amazing? Keep stating it out loud and practicing it and like anything you do over and over again, it will become part of you and call forth the powerful wonders of God's favor daily.

THE PRAYER OF SURRENDER

This is a sample prayer that you can pray to surrender your fear. This is just a template for you to build upon as you prepare to cast out fear once and for all.

Heavenly Father, in the name of Jesus,

I thank you and praise you for all you are and all you are doing in my life. Thank you for being such an awesome and mighty God. Lord, I thank you for the many, many blessings you have bestowed upon me. I thank you for every triumph and challenge I have experienced that leads me closer to you. Lord, I confess that I have been experiencing fear. I have been fearful about [list your fears.] I know that in order to move forward, it is time to release this fear. Lord, I have done all that I know to do and I am asking for your help.

I know that all things are possible through Christ who strengthens me. I am standing in my power as your child and I release this fear right now. I surrender this fear to you, God, and call forth faith in every aspect of my life, in the name of Jesus. Lord, in the name of Jesus, let your signs and wonders accompany me as I minister and live your vision. Father, in the name of Jesus, I ask you for [list the desires of your heart] so I can fulfill your high calling on my life. I thank you for fulfilling my every need and providing all that I need to live your will. All this I pray in Jesus' name, Amen.

Tweak your *Prayer of Surrender* in a way that works for you and begin saying it to yourself *every* morning in your devotion and quiet time until becomes a part of your reality.

Chapter Six

The Power of Being Saved

Note: This chapter only pertains to you if you are not saved. If you are clear of your salvation, feel free to proceed to Chapter Seven, Is Your Heart Ready for God?

When God introduced this work to me through Frank and Ida Hammond's book, *Pigs in the Parlor*, I distinctly remember a part of the book where Mr. Hammond responded to the question, "Can someone who is not saved be delivered?" He answered, "Why would you deliver someone who is not saved?"

I thought that was very harsh at the time. Now I have a better understanding of why He said that. I have come to understand that it is not fair to deliver someone who has not given their life to Jesus Christ because they have no access to the authority of Jesus and therefore, the Holy Spirit. It may set them up for unclean spirits coming back with a vengeance. Matthew 12:43 - 45 reminds us that when evil spirits come back and find that the Holy Spirit is not present within them, they will bring spirits seven times worse than themselves and they will be in worse shape than when they began this process. That is what I mean by it being unfair.

Any spirit within any person will only bow to the name of Jesus. Unless someone is born again, I don't recommend that they go through this work. If they already have a mess on their hands, they may have an even larger mess if they attempt to move in authority they have not been granted through Christ Jesus.

The real question is, why *would* you want to live without the covering and power of Jesus? It wasn't until I began to do this work that I received true revelation of the words Jesus Christ shared, "I am the way, the truth, and the life: no man cometh unto the Father, but by me (John 14:6)." There is no other name to which unclean spirits bow because there is no other god than the Son of God who came, experienced death and was resurrected to defeat the acts of Satan.

> *There is no other name than Jesus to which unclean spirits bow.*

Therefore, God by any other name will not work beyond giving you a short-term emotional high. There is no other way to get everlasting and eternal life but through Jesus Christ. Keep reading because if you are not saved and would like to experience the fullness of this work, I will walk you through the process of becoming saved so you can read on knowing that you have full access to the one true God.

My Journey to Jesus

I want to share a bit more about my spiritual journey so you can understand that while I have respect for other religions and spiritual beliefs, they cannot even come near the power of understanding Jesus. Jesus came to save everyone, but not everyone lives with the benefits of being saved if they have not received Jesus as their Lord and Savior. Then, once you are saved, you must ask to be filled with the Holy Spirit so you can be born again and be led into all Truth.

As I write these words, last Sunday when my daughter and I were at Zion Christian Training Center's Sunday class Apostle

Forte was teaching that being born again is beyond being saved and the true goal of Christians.

He was sharing how you know whether or not someone is truly filled with the Holy Spirit. It goes beyond them just speaking in tongues, attending church, and knowing the Word; they actually have to be deeply moving toward living righteously. When you are filled with The Holy Spirit, you simply cannot easily sin or live in unclean ways. Anyone who professes to be a Christian and repeatedly defiles themselves dishonors God's gifts in their life.

> But the things that come out of the mouth come from the heart, and these make a man 'unclean.' For out of the heart come evil thoughts, murder, adultery, sexual immorality, theft, false testimony, slander. These are what make a man 'unclean'... - Matthew 15:18 – 20.

Anyone who participates in this behavior is not filled with the Holy Ghost. When the Holy Spirit is within you, you no longer live in iniquity (leaning toward sin), you live in righteousness (living above sin). The two lifestyles simply cannot co-exist.

It is possible to know God and still be turned over to unrighteousness as you can see from the behavior of far too many Christians. But it is not possible to be filled with the Holy Spirit and move in such darkness as in the following verses.

> Furthermore, since they did not think it worthwhile to retain the knowledge of God, He gave them over to a depraved mind, to do what ought not to be done.
>
> They have become filled with every kind of wickedness, evil, greed and depravity. They are full of envy, murder, strife, deceit and malice. They are gossips, slanderers, God-haters, insolent, arrogant and boastful; they invent ways of doing evil; they

disobey their parents; they are senseless, faithless, heartless, ruthless.

Although they know God's righteous decree that those who do such things deserve death, they not only continue to do these very things but also approve of those who practice them. – Romans 1: 28 – 31 KJ

As Apostle was teaching, my daughter leaned over and whispered to me, "How do you become born again?'" I told her to ask him and she did. He answered that you become born again by asking the Holy Spirit to fill you and then you allow your old life to die and feed your new life through prayer, fasting, reading the Word, and asking God to reveal Himself to you.

On our way home that day she said to me, "Mama, we have to keep coming back because I need to make sure I am going to Heaven." If you know you are going to Heaven and have access to God's Kingdom on earth because you are saved and born again, you can certainly skip this part of the book and go right to Chapter Six. If you are not 100% certain or need to rededicate your life to Jesus, read on.

Are You Ready To Be Saved?

We so often hear the choice of becoming saved associated with knowing where you are going when you pass on. Being saved is not only about knowing you are going to Heaven when it is your time, it is also about having access to the power of Jesus right now in your life. You can only take your rightful place in the Heavenly rank and operate in the fullness of the power of God when you make the choice to be saved.

Being saved brings the process to clarify your life's purpose and calling. You have now set yourself apart as someone who seeks to live as a child or offspring of God. Being saved is the doorway through which God begins to teach you, clean you out and transform your life into the life He has for you, which is far better than anything you can think or imagine for yourself. If you are ready to have a clear understanding of what God created for you to do and to learn your specific Kingdom assignment, then you are ready to be saved.

The first step in the process of being born again is to accept Jesus Christ as your Lord and Savior. You do this by taking a few minutes and just accessing the areas of sin or iniquity in your life. Not in a point-the-finger-at-yourself-and-give-yourself-a-lecture kind of way, but in a loving, open, and honest way.

- Have you had enough of trying to make your life work by the world's standards?

- Are you ready to experience a whole new reality that gives you access to all God has for you?

- Are you ready to begin the not-always-easy process of putting down your old self and picking up the Self Jesus has for you?

- Are you ready to get into position for the reward of God and His mysteries to be opened up to you?

- Are you ready to begin again and be free from your past sins?

If you answered yes to these questions, you are ready to be saved.

You are ready to be saved.

If you are ready to take the first step toward being born again, getting saved, then simply pray the following Prayer of Salvation. This prayer decrees and declares that you belong to Jesus and He is now your covering. It is more about opening your heart to God then it is about the Words of the prayer itself, so you can speak from your heart and desire for God to reveal Himself to you. He is now about to plant His Kingdom within you and will teach you how to become His temple and live a life that fully supports who you are in Him.

Jesus said "Come to me, all you who are weary and burdened, and I will give you rest (Matthew 11:28). Just as you are, right where you are you can come to Jesus. Come with all of your questions, concerns, and past sinful choices. He died for you and loves you just as you are.

Here is what you need to do:

1. Realize that you have sinned and fallen short of the glory of God. You have been trying to live without Jesus Christ, and when you do this, you have no way out of sin. Now you have a way to live above sin.

2. Acknowledge that you realize that Jesus Christ died on the cross for *you*. He gave His life for *you* so you might live and manifest all who He created you to be. He died so you can take your rightful place above Satan, sin and the world.

3. Repent of your sin. To repent means more than just confessing, it means to "turn away from." It means to change your direction in life. To sin is to turn away from God, to repent is to turn to God.

4. Receive Jesus Christ into your life. Receiving Jesus Christ is not just about going through the actions of church or trying to be good, it is about opening your heart to Jesus so He can use you as His temple to hold His Holy Spirit and do the works He created you to do for His glory. Receiving Jesus Christ means that He takes up residence in your life and heart and body.

5. Pray the following Prayer of Salvation.

THE PRAYER OF SALVATION

Father, in the name of Jesus,

I come to you as humble as I know how, confessing that I *have sinned and fallen short of your glory over and over in my life. Today, I am choosing to turn away from the sinful life I have been leading and turn to the life you have for me. I now believe that You died for me so I might live above sin and take hold of the life you have for me.*

I give my heart to you. I give my mind to you. I give my soul to you. I open my heart to receiving the love you have for me. I open my mind to your teachings and the truth about who You are and who I am in you. I lay down my ways so you can instruct me in Your ways.

I receive you as my personal Lord and Savior. You are now the head of my life. Lord, please teach me how to yield to you, how to hear from you, and how to obey You. Please teach me Your ways. I now engraft myself to you and move forward in my life, producing good fruit.

Lord, allow me to touch the lives you created me to touch. Use me Lord as you teach me so that I might live a life that reflects You everywhere I go and in all that I am doing.

Lord, please show me how to move in the authority, power, and dominion that you intended for all who belong to you. Please fill me with Your Holy Spirit so I can truly know you and recognize your voice. Thank you, Lord, for saving me and becoming my Father. Amen.

Once you have prayed this Prayer of Salvation, then the next steps are to:

1. Get a copy of the Bible that is in a version that you understand. Begin to spend time daily in the Word. I would suggest beginning in Proverbs in the Old Testament and Matthew in the New Testament.

2. Keep a list of questions you would like to have answered about God, your faith, the Bible, etc. You can begin to go on a Bible website (I use biblegateway.com), enter your topics of interest and read all of the scripture pertaining to that topic in the Word. Ask God to open up your understanding of His Word.

3. Spend time daily in your Bible, sitting still and asking God the questions you have for Him. Wait for His answers.

4. Find a church home that teaches the Word and also teaches you how to discover and move in God's vision for your life.

Chapter Seven

Is Your Heart Ready For God?

I took my thirteen year old daughter out to eat at Red Robin for Valentine's Day this past February and she told me that I embarrass her because it seems like I'm drunk all the time. Her comment just cracked me up because I cannot recall that last time I even had a drink.

I knew she was referring to my overflowing joy that keeps me grinning from ear-to-ear, randomly laughing out loud and spontaneously singing off-key songs of praise and worship wherever I am. I suppose it does look like I'm crazy and drunk to a thirteen year-old.

I thought to myself, "If she only knew what God has brought me through and how the fact that I have a clean heart is a miracle." Remembering being hurt by men so many times that I stopped counting, having a father who criticized me three times for every one time he encouraged me, having to leave friendships behind, and my daughter's father marrying another woman while I was 3 months pregnant with his child, brought on yet another random burst of laughter as I am so thankful that God showed me the steps to fully heal my heart – no matter what.

While I began doing emotional healing work twenty years ago, God has more recently brought me a full understanding of just how important our hearts are to Him. Your heart was designed to be clear and free for God to use you to fulfill His purpose in your life. Without forgiveness, no matter how many times you go to the altar or how many times a minister lays hands on you for deliverance, you cannot be fully delivered.

When your heart has even a remnant of unforgiveness, resentment or emotional hurt still lingering, it leaves God less capacity to work with. As if that is not enough reason to heal, the other critical reason you must forgive is that unforgiveness is food and sustenance for unclean spirits. The first step to getting them out of your temple is for you to remove their food – to literally starve them out.

God created your heart to be able to hear from Him, to love and to desire the things of God. Your heart was created for the purpose of bringing forth the fruits of the Holy Spirit, and it must be clean to do this.

A clean heart has no resentment, emotional pain, hurt, suffering, anger, or bitterness whatsoever. Whether you have been hurt from past romantic relationships, friendships, family, church members, or sexual violation, you can have a heart free of heaviness and pain – a clean heart.

It is possible to have a clean heart, it is a requirement for you to move into all God has for you.

> For if you forgive men when they sin against you, your heavenly Father will also forgive you. But if you do not forgive men their sins, your Father will not forgive your sins. – Matthew 6:14 - 15

God has literally created a tablet in your heart that can either be filled with clean things or unclean things (Proverbs 7:3). It also shows that while you can appear to the world to laugh and be okay, your heart can still ache from past hurts (Proverbs 14:13). Unforgiveness literally blocks your blessings. A clean heart is a requirement to fully love and serve God. God has shown me seven steps to experience the emotional wholeness He has for you. After twenty years of witnessing these steps transform lives, I want to share them with you. This piece has to be in place in order to experience your complete deliverance.

The Seven Steps to Emotional Healing

Yes, there is a process to clean your heart and release all emotional baggage that is hindering you. With the following steps, you can erase emotional baggage once and for all:

1. Allow yourself to feel.
2. Confess.
3. Understand what you made it mean.
4. Identify the unforgiveness and release it.
5. Choose to forgive.
6. Pray! Pray! Pray!
7. Make a new choice and walk in it.

These steps work without fail when you follow them. Once your heart is clean, you can keep it that way by remembering to go through these steps every time something occurs that causes you emotional hurt so your heart remains clean and fully available to God.

Allow Yourself to Feel

I developed these steps to emotional healing long before the emotional challenge of my life hit me. When I was three months pregnant with my daughter, her father – whom I spent a great deal of time with and was considering marrying – told me that he was getting married to another woman the next morning. You can only imagine that I felt like I had been hit by a Mack truck.

It definitely presented the opportunity for me to put these steps to emotional healing to a much deeper test. I decided that even with the excruciating emotional pain that I was experiencing, I would not allow anyone to have the power to decide if I would love and be loved in the future.

I remember being afraid to allow myself to really feel what I was dealing with. I was afraid that I would start crying and never be able to stop. I was also afraid that feeling my pain would get in the way of taking care of my daughter and daily obligations. I decided to trust God and keep moving through the steps to emotional healing so I could be whole. There is no other way.

The next step to your healing is to fully realize the depth of the pain you are feeling. When you allow yourself to feel it, you are beginning the process of becoming free. How badly did it hurt? Where do you carry the pain? When is your hurt the most challenging for you?

Despite what you might have heard, healing has nothing to do with time. You can only heal to the extent that you acknowledge and deal with your pain.

Confess

It is very easy to be busy every day of your life and never fully comprehend that you are in emotional pain. Living this way locks you out of God's promises.

It is very easy to be busy every day of your life and never fully comprehend that you are in emotional pain.

Until you first acknowledge and admit that unhealed emotional pain is present in your life, you will be unable to be free from it. You must first acknowledge that incomplete pain is present. Confess each area in which this incomplete pain has been allowed to affect your decisions and life.

What Did You Make It Mean?

The true power of healing lies in understanding the difference between the face of what actually happened and what you made it mean. When the father of my unborn baby told me he was marring another woman the next morning, I had a good, deep heaving cry and then set out to begin my healing process.

This was no easy task because I made his marrying mean so many negative things about me and my ability to have and keep a loving man. I made it mean that I wasn't good enough (this one was one I was already struggling with, so his choice was like pouring salt into an open wound). I made it mean that I must not be attractive; I did not know how to keep a man; I could not sustain a relationship; I didn't deserve to have someone there to help me raise my child; it must have been something I did; and the list went on and on.

I knew from doing this work that I could only heal to the extent that I stopped making this experience mean all of those things. I literally took the fact that he was getting married (oh, and did I mention that I found out the night before he was getting married?) and I *Velcro-ed* my own negative meanings to the facts of what happened.

I decided to allow this to be an isolated event in my life. I knew that God must have really been trying to get my attention and although it hurt like crazy then, I would one day be grateful that I did not marry someone who had the character to do what he did.

I can now look back and thank God over and over again. He was not the man for me. While we have a good relationship now and he is a part of my daughter's life, God had something much better in mind for me and knew that I need a special man to walk with me on the path that God chose for me.

Did you know that it is not the fact of what happened that actually creates emotional pain? It is what you added to the fact that hurts.

It is not the fact of what actually happened that actually creates emotional pain, it is what you added to the fact that hurts.

Once you have identified the people and the situations you are holding on to, it is time to uncover what you made it mean about yourself so you can create a new pattern of living once your heart is healed. This exercise holds much emotional healing power in it. Please make sure you stop and actually do the work. Reading over these questions will not be enough to complete your healing.

Here are some questions that you can ask yourself to uncover what you have attached to past situations. Use this worksheet for each individual hurt you are working on healing (I suggest you make copies or use a separate sheet of paper).

Think of each specific occurrence or situation that created emotional pain for you. Then ask yourself the following questions:

What did you make what happened mean about yourself?

_____

_____

_____

_____

What conclusions did you draw about yourself?

_____

_____

_____

_____

What did you attach or Velcro to what happened?

_____

_____

_____

_____

How are you punishing yourself? How are you sabotaging yourself?

_____

_____

_____

_____

Identify The Unforgiveness and Release It

Now that you have separated the fact of what actually happened from what you made it mean, you can complete the process of cleaning your heart. When the Holy Spirit was bringing this process to me, although I had been working in the area of emotional healing for eighteen years, He added a step that is critical to experiencing more of God.

I used to think that we held onto pain in relation to the person. For example, if you had issues with your mother, you could stand at the altar and declare that you forgive your mother and that would cover everything she'd ever done that hurt you. Then, as I was praying for the total process of deliverance, the Holy Spirit shared with me that we actually hold on to pain by situation and not by the person.

This means that you not only identify the person who hurt you, you list every incident that wounded your heart. The most difficult person of all to forgive is yourself. *Remember to add yourself on the end of your list.*

I have included an example to get you started. First, make a list of everyone toward whom you are still holding on to past hurts, pains, anger and resentment. Once you have your list, use the following format to then list out what it is that they did that left you hurt or emotionally wounded.

I suggest that you do this on separate pieces of paper so you have all of the space you need. I usually end up filling up anywhere from five to six sheets of full-size paper for each person with whom I walk through this exercise. Here is a sample of the exercise:

The Person

What They Did

my mother, Joan

For not teaching me about men. For working all the time and not giving me the attention I needed and wanted. For never telling me I was smart.

Once you have listed the specific things you have been holding on to, it is time to verbally forgive. It is a requirement to this process that you do it out loud. Remember, Satan is the prince of the air, and he and his minions hear (Ephesians 2:2). When you verbally speak your choice of forgiveness, he has to cross that thing off the list of what his unclean spirits can feed on. It sounds strange, but it is absolutely true.

Using my example above, you would say out loud, "I forgive Mama for never telling me I was smart and beautiful." Then, "I forgive Mama for not teaching me about men." Then, "I forgive Mama for working so hard and not giving me the attention I needed and wanted." Speak each one separately until you feel that you have honestly let it go. Then, move on to the next person. This could take awhile, I know, but it is worth it.

No matter how much forgiveness work you have done in the past, go through this entire process without skipping any portion. Your heart is the key to Jesus opening up His Kingdom to you and this work cannot be underestimated.

Again, the specific steps are:

1. On one sheet of paper, make a list of all the people toward whom you are still holding on to bitterness, anger, resentment or emotional hurt.

2. On a second sheet of paper, write out the specific instances, circumstances or behaviors you have been holding on to in regards to each person on your list.

3. Speak the full statement of forgiveness out loud for each person for each listed instance, circumstance, or behavior.

Pray! Pray! Pray!

In the midst of your healing process, make sure that you take time to get in touch with God and the fact that you are a child of God. Give your burden to God. Release it. Ask God to take the pain from your heart and spirit. He will. You can wake up the next day and no longer have that raw, heavy, feeling of hurt and pain.

For years I would take myself through the steps to emotional healing and I did not have this one on the list because over time, the steps worked. Then at yet another time of emotional devastation (I have lost count of how many times I have had to use these steps – thank God!) I decided that I wanted to get over it almost immediately and with no emotional residue or scarring. I knew it was possible because healing has no relation to the amount of time that passes since being hurt.

It dawned on me to simply ask God to remove the feeling of heaviness and pain I was carrying around. The most amazing thing happened – overnight the hurt disappeared. This step then became a critical part of this healing process. I included a heart healing prayer at the end of the chapter for you. Once you have prayed, you then make the choice to forgive.

Choose to Forgive

Forgiveness is a choice. It has nothing to do with the amount of time that passes, it has to do with choice. Forgiveness is not about the other person involved, it about you getting your whole heart back. You have to accept that the other person or people involved may never get to a place to ask for your forgiveness and it still does not affect your ability to forgive. Declare that you choose to forgive yourself and the others involved.

Forgiveness is a choice.

Make a New Choice and Walk in it

The next step is to re-program yourself to redefine your reality. You get to make a new choice and decide who you are going to be from this moment forward and walk in it. You can refer back to your unforgiveness list and your list of what you made those past painful experiences mean about yourself.

You now need to come up with new choices that fit where you would like to be emotionally. For example, if you made a past hurt mean that you may not ever find someone you can trust, you would retool it to say something like, "God will bless me with someone who I can trust to love, and who protects and adores me." The key is that is has to be more positively powerful than the negative belief was. This is tedious heart work, but it is necessary to truly clean your heart.

Now that your heart is cleaned, you are ready to move forward in this process. You are on your way...

A PRAYER FOR YOU

Heavenly Father, in the name of Jesus, today is a new day. This moment is a new moment and from this moment forward I choose to live a healed life. Your Word says that you will replace my heart of stone with a heart of flesh and I am standing on your Word right now. Lord, your Word says that you will give me a clean heart and a right spirit and I now receive a new heart that is free of emotional pain from my past.

Today, I forgive myself for any past choices that led to pain and anyone else who has caused me pain in my life. I lay down any hurt, malice, bitterness, judgment, anger, hatred or wrath. I pick up love, joy, gentleness, meekness, kindness, faithfulness and sound mind. I forgive them and I pray your blessings upon them that they will be healed and whole so they experience your love as I do. I remove from the tablet of my heart anything that is in the way of me hearing and seeing clearly from you.

My heart is now free to hear from you and to show others the love that your word commands of me. I now know that I am lovable, special and adorable and I open up to receiving love from you through others. I no longer have to guard my heart as it is clean and clear and able to clearly discern what I need to see in people. By your stripes, I am healed.

From this moment forward, I will only allow the love and joy in my heart to speak through my lips. I speak love over my life and all the lives with whom I come in contact. My heart is open to receive the immeasurable blessings and inheritance from Jesus Christ, my Lord and Savior. – In Jesus' name, Amen.

Chapter Eight

The Stronghold Spirits and Their Fruit

One of the greatest lies perpetuated by Satan is that once you accept Christ as your Lord and Savior, you then are completely cleansed of all unclean spirits. That is not true. While becoming saved gives you access to be cleaned through Jesus Christ and forgives you of the sin and unclean habits that you may have had in your life, it does not mean that anything is cast out. Being saved does not mean being cleansed of unclean spirits.

Being saved does not mean being cleansed of unclean spirits.

Being saved does not get rid of the many unclean spirits that found their way into your temple when you were in the world. You must become clean through deliverance, the deliberate removal of unclean spirits.

I have been to many, many church services as I travel the country and have observed preachers getting the congregation emotionally riled-up and declaring that deliverance is happening. Not true. The same unclean spirits that were inside of them when they came in leave with them when they walk out.

spiritual war; earthly war

There is no more spiritual warfare.

There is no more spiritual warfare. Christians only have to step into their full power, dominion and authority and subdue Satan. The spiritual war to defeat Satan occurred before the foundation of the earth was laid, so it is no longer Satan we battle against. The earthly war to defeat Satan was won the instant Jesus died on the cross. Jesus defeated Satan and his works (I John 3:8).

Your struggle is now against holding your faith and being fully aware of who you are in Jesus. Once you are certain of your Heavenly rank, there is no stronghold that can stand against you. You have everything you need to remove every single stronghold from your life forever. II Corinthians 10:3 – 4 clearly reminds you that you already have the divine power to demolish every stronghold and move beyond Satan to the living the higher things of Jesus.

> For though we live in the world, we do no wage war as the world does. The weapons we fight with are not the weapons of the world. On the contrary, they have divine power to demolish strongholds.

The problem is that you have not understood the stronghold spirits or how they manifest in your life. After reading this chapter, you will be clear about each of the strongholds and what they produce in your life. You will know what they are named and how to demolish them once and for all.

This is the part of this work to which Mary Garrison's book, *How To Try A Spirit: By Their Fruits You Will Know Them* truly brought understanding and revelation (and I was six years old when she wrote it!). Ms. Garrison shares that God put here in total communion with Him or "Holy Spirit School," as she describes it, to reveal this work to her. "Holy Spirit School" was the same, exact term I used to describe the way God brought this work to me. It was confirmation.

It was this work that the Holy Spirit showed her that provided the breakthrough to knowing that identifying the strong man or stronghold spirit is the key. While it appears that there are an unlimited number of unclean spirits, the truth is that there are a limited number of unclean stronghold spirits that can manifest their fruit in many ways.

> Or again, how can anyone enter a strong man's house and carry off his possessions unless he first ties up the strong man? Then he can rob his house. – Matthew 12:29

In my attempts to contact Ms. Garrison through her daughter, she shared her concern that over the years, many people had simply taken her work, created charts, and called it their own. I want to be very careful to give her groundbreaking work all of the credit it truly deserves and add the pieces that the Holy Spirit has shown me since I first began moving in cleaning hearts and spirits.

While the strongholds came from Ms. Garrison's work, some of the fruits of the strongholds are those that the Holy Spirit has added through me. I have also added explanations as I have come to understand or encounter them to both Mrs. Garrison's original listings and those that I have added.

Stronghold Spirits

I want to explain how I have laid out this section so you can maximize your results. You will find lists of each unclean spirit and their fruit or manifestations below their name. There is a check box next to each fruit or manifestation. As you read through each stronghold and its fruit, check the manifestations that you have been experiencing.

When you check a box under a stronghold spirit, it means that this spirit, at some time in your life, found an open door and made its way into your temple to attempt to stop you from bringing forth all God has for you. Following the checklists, I have included description of the fruit with examples of it shows up in your life, so you can be crystal clear about what you have been dealing with.

Suspend any judgment and remember that most of these unclean spirits found their way in without your conscious knowledge. You will want to understand when the door was opened for them to enter, but do not be overly concerned. You just need to get them out so you can have all of your life back.

When the stronghold spirit is cast out, the fruit or its manifestations also leave your life. You will stop the behaviors and habits that the stronghold spirit is responsible for planting and expressing in your temple and therefore your life.

The Fruit

My father, Nat, is a businessman who wears suits and ties by day and an agriculturist who wears boots, work overalls and lumberjack shirts by night. It has become a mainstay for him to be outside well into the wee hours of the night on his tractor landscaping, cutting wood, or just playing on his many acres of land.

There are apple and pear trees growing on his beloved land and he often boasts of how much he loves being able to eat his own pesticide-free and plentiful fruit. When the fruit is in season, he picks the fruit from the branches, wipes them on his work shirt and bites into them.

Whenever I think of the fruit of unclean spirits, I think of my parents' apple and pear trees. You can identify unclean spiritual fruit in your life and attempt to cast it out, but you will only get temporary results. Then the fruit will return.

This happens because you have not gotten rid of the spiritual "tree" or the stronghold spirit responsible for growing the fruit in the first place. Just as my father can keep removing damaged apples or pears from the tree branches, he must pull the tree up by the roots to get rid of the problem or the issues will keep coming back. You recognize the stronghold spirit by the fruit it produces.

> *By their fruit you will recognize them. Do people pick grapes from thornbushes, or figs from thistles? Likewise every good tree bears good fruit, but a bad tree bears bad fruit. A good tree cannot bear bad fruit, and a bad tree cannot bear good fruit. ¹⁹Every tree that does not bear good fruit is cut down and thrown into the fire. Thus, by their fruit you will recognize them. – Matthew 7:16 – 20*

> *Make a tree good and its fruit will be good, or make a tree bad and its fruit will be bad, for a tree is recognized by its fruit. – Matthew 12:33*

It works the same way in the spiritual realm with stronghold spirits and unclean fruit. Unclean stronghold spirits can only produce unclean fruit (Luke 6:43 - 44). A bad tree can only produce bad fruit. It is impossible for it to work any other way. That also means that if you want to dismiss unclean fruit from your life once and for all, you must understand which spiritual tree is growing it and remove that tree all together. That is what this portion of this work walks you through.

It is imperative that you recognize any fruits that have manifested in your life so you can call them out by name in your lives and those God will send you to deliver. I go into detail with each fruit because it is too easy to just read a fruit and think it doesn't pertain to you.

For now, it is time to become familiar with the fruit so you can identify the stronghold spirit responsible for creating it in your life. I teach you how to cast out the fruit in the following chapter. As you read these fruit and their descriptions, I pray that you have "Aha!" moment after "Aha!" moment like I did when I first began to understand what you are about to learn. It's time to open up your understanding.

Here we go...

THE SPIRIT OF FEAR

When I first opened my Twitter account, I began to follow certain people to see how they used Twitter. One of the people I followed was Tony Robbins, the famous motivational speaker. One day I received a "tweet" from him that said that fear and faith are both unseen and made up. I replied, "Fear is a spirit and it is very real. It is not imagined and must be dealt with accordingly". I think I got kicked off of his Twitter account for good. This reminded me just how misunderstood fear has been.

Fear has been one of the most misunderstood areas and the topic of countless books, workshops and entire conferences. I pray that this part of the book along completes your understanding of fear and how to be freed from it for good.

If you have not read Chapter Four, *Your Fearless Foundation,* stop here and go back and read that chapter. It is imperative that you first understand what fear is and why God allows it before you proceed with this section.

The Fruit of the Spirit of Fear

- ☑ Dread
- ☑ Doubt *leads to double-mindedness*
- ☑ Procrastination
- ☐ Hesitation
- ☐ Emotional Barriers
- ☑ Lack of clarity of vision
- ☑ Torment
- ☑ Faithlessness/Lack of belief
- ☐ Fear of Death
- ☑ Nightmares
- ☑ Apprehension *fear of future trouble or evil*
- ☑ Anxiety *close to 'apprehension*
- ☑ Cowardice/Being Overly Cautious
- ☑ Intimidation/Fear of Man
- ☑ Worry
- ? ☑ Shyness/Timidity
- ☑ Inadequacy *can be repaired after fear cast out.*
- ☑ Tension/Stress
- ☐ Heart Attacks
- ☐ Fear of poverty
- ☑ Phobias *spiders, heights*
- ☐ Nervousness
- ☐ Overanalyzing

How the Spirit of Fear Enters

The spirit of fear has been allowed to live with us for so many generations; it has just become the norm or commonplace. If you think back as far as you can, you can probably recall fear your parents experienced when attempting to live out their dreams and purpose. They would probably be able to recall the fear that their parents felt and it could go on for generations.

Fear is one of Satan's most powerful tools to keep you limited and disobedient to the voice of God in your life. The Spirit of fear often teams with a lying spirit to convince you that you are not the one for the vision God has shown you.

The door through which this stronghold enters is opened when you do not obey the instruction of God. From there, there is a snowball effect until you may easily talk yourself out of even doing little things that will improve your life and move God's purpose forward.

Dread

You experience this fruit of fear when you have serious resistance to moving forward in your life. It can be that you are afraid of the unknown, failure, success, what people might think or say or losing friends as you move on to new successes. It may be that you are not being obedient to what God tells you to do because you are dreading that people will not show up once you put in all of the work to manifest your vision.

Once I committed to moving forward in my vision, I had to overcome dread. I remember being on a coaching call with my coach, Jennifer, and she asked me what I was afraid of. I replied, "I am afraid that I will put all this work into this vision and it will be ready to launch and I will step out onto stage, and no one will be in the audience. It will be like...'Introducing...Ericka D. Jackson...' and I will step out from behind the thick red curtain and every chair in the audience will be empty. Not only will they be empty, I would hear the sound of crickets just to remind me of how empty it is."

We both laughed at the imagery, but it was very real for me at the time. She helped me process through it and each and every time I have put something out to my flock they have responded in a wonderful way.

Dread can often come up for you if you have imagined everything that you think you have to change in your life to be successful. Once I got over my initial dread, the next one I had to deal with was imagining that once I shared this work with the world, I would then be even more tired and have no time to do anything I wanted to do. I was already feeling stretched too thin with all that was on my plate and the thought of having more speaking engagements, appointments, obligations and responsibilities used to leave me dreading what I *thought* success would look like.

It turns out I was wrong. As I move to new levels (and I'm just getting started), I actually have more people wanting to help and more resources to get some of the things I used to have to do myself off of my plate. The truth is that the more I put this work God created in me out in the world, the more people see the anointing on the work and the more they offer to help free me up so I can focus on the work, and not the distractions that are part of everyday living.

Just last night, a minister asked me how I was doing. I shared with her that I was feeling a bit tired and was trying to figure out how to get some things off of my plate. With God expanding the work of the ministry and still being a single mother (all of those parents who told me that a teenaged child requires more of your time and energy were right – whew!), it takes it's toll on me from time to time. I mentioned how much of a challenge it is for everything to fall on my shoulders. She mentioned that she would be happy to grocery shop for me, loved to cook, and would be happy to come over and do some cooking for us. Wow! I was reminded again of just how much time is needlessly spent conjuring up all of the aspects of success that aren't even true.

Doubt *(word of God)*

Doubt occurs when you have been given an idea or have been instructed to do something by God and after feeling somewhat sure of it at first, you allow yourself to come up with reasons it might not work. You sabotage yourself and fail to follow through on the idea or instruction. This type is doubt is mentioned in the Word in Matthew 14:31 and Matthew 21:21.

You can also doubt the Word of God. This occurs when you read the Word or hear a sermon, feel good for that day and as soon as a challenge arises, you doubt or forget that God's word works without fail. The minute you doubt, it erases the power of the Word to move in your life (Matthew 28:17; Mark 11:23).

Double-mindedness

Once doubt creeps in, you then move into double-mindedness. This occurs when you are literally going back-and-forth in your mind trying to both convince yourself of something and talk yourself out of something. "I can do it, there is no reason why God won't help me," may be one thought quickly followed by, "This isn't going to work! I don't have a clue as to how to do this. I can't do this at all."

You can find yourself literally going back-and-forth for years and never take the necessary steps to have your breakthrough. Double-mindedness also shows up as indecisiveness or an inability to make decisions quickly and effectively. James 1:8 reminds you that, "A double-minded man in unstable in all he does."

Procrastination

Procrastination is not supposed to be part of the human experience. I actually used to think so until I began to observe people who did not procrastinate. My mother is not a procrastinator. She has a favorite seat she sits in and gets a particular look on her face when she is thinking of her days and weeks to come. She sits and makes lists to capture her thoughts and then executes her lists with amazing accuracy, always ahead of time.

My father is the worst possible procrastinator. He should have a doctorate degree in procrastinating. Prior to my spirit being cleaned, I walked the scary line between both of my parents. I am a true planner and list-maker, but I would jam way too much in, and end up procrastinating.

Procrastination is not a part of your personality, even if you have procrastinated as far back as elementary school. That just means that the spirit of fear has been with you awhile. It is possible to live in a way that you do not procrastinate and you actually bring things forth with ease, and without pushing at the last minute.

Even if you have convinced yourself that you are a "pinch player," and you work best under pressure, it is not the Truth. You may be used to working under pressure due to your habit of procrastinating, but it is not how God created you.

Procrastination is a different issue than literally having too much on your plate and not enough time to get to it. That is a time management issue or evidence of you not being able to say "No" to people. Procrastinators wait until the last minute even if they have more than enough time and opportunity to complete something on time or well in advance.

God created a time for everything and a season for every activity under heaven (Ecclesiastes 3:1). If you feel like you are a chronic procrastinator, it is a sign that there is an unclean spirit present, keeping you off course. I know that is deep, but it is true. Let's keep moving...

Hesitation

Perhaps you have experienced hesitation and weren't even aware that it isn't how you were created. Anytime you have been instructed by God to say something to someone or He has put a feeling in you to act on and you hold back or put off the action, you are hesitating.

Emotional Barriers

"No one will ever hurt me again..."

"I will never let anyone get that close to me again," or, "I don't ever want to put myself in a position for anyone to use me again." These are all statements you may have thought at sometime if you are experiencing emotional barriers.

Emotional barriers are walls or guards you erect around your heart and in your life to seemingly protect yourself from potential emotional pain. While emotional barriers can also enter through the stronghold of the spirit of bondage, most emotional barriers originate out of a fear of being hurt, based on past unforgiveness.

Emotional barriers are rooted in the fear of being hurt. The challenge with emotional barriers is that you actually get trapped inside of their walls and are unable to experience love. You were not designed to live with emotional barriers. Your previous work on releasing emotional baggage should have proven to you that no matter what, you can always return your heart to being fully cleansed and whole. Now that you know those steps, casting out the spirit of fear will enable you to be fully free from holding yourself back from the love God created you to experience.

Torment

When someone is tormented, it goes far beyond occasional disturbance to the intense affliction of great pain, bodily harm, mental suffering, or annoyance. As I was doing an initial consultation with a client named Sharon, she shared what she wanted to rid her life of through *A Clean Sweep*™. She described literally being bothered by "little green men" that she clearly saw when she was a child. While this may sound crazy at first glance, upon closer examination it is just part of how Satan attempts to get to you.

She has a mighty calling on her life, and it did not surprise me that she had experienced torment from the time she was a child. While you may not have experienced little green men, you may have endured certain thoughts, fears, phobias, memories, or dreams that pick at your mind, body or spirit and seem like they are out of your control. This is what it feels like to be tormented.

[handwritten margin note: Torment from childhood]

Faithlessness/Lack of Belief

When you have the presence of the spirit of fear in your life, it is impossible to be faithful. The opposite of fear is faith. When you are dealing with the spirit of fear, your faith is literally choked-out. You are unable to believe God for the very things you desire and He promises in the Word. You remain stuck in hoping and wishing and feel helpless as to how to get yourself back into a space of belief.

Faith is the substance God responds to. He does not respond to your tears. Faithlessness must be eliminated or it overflows into all areas of your life.

Fear of Death

My friend Toni and I have this saying when something is so deep it leaves you speechless. We call it "getting the teeth knocked out of your head." When we share deep stories, it won't be long before one of us says, "Girl...my teeth just fell out." This is a deep one, and what I say may knock your teeth out. Are you ready?

Satan was granted the power over death by God Himself. When Jesus died on the cross, he freed us from death through His name. He literally gave us the power *over* death. If you do not doubt, you have the ability to call people back from the dead and to rebuke Satan from causing people to die. God is a miracle-working God and He left you all of the keys you need to not die, but to be translated, like Enoch. Believers are not to die of sickness or issues with our physical body, but only when Jesus transcribes us from this life into heaven (Genesis 5:24).

You only fear death when you do not fully understand that, through Jesus, you literally have power over death. Remember, Satan can only enter your life with permission and you have the power through Jesus to stop Satan and all unclean spirits from showing up in your life. Circumstances that lead to death are actually the workings of Satan's unclean spirits. When the fear of death leaves, you will be able to truly live. I told you it might knock out your teeth.

Nightmares

Anyone who has experienced a nightmare needs no explanation. They are dreams that literally scare you in your sleep and leave you waking up in a cold sweat and your heart beating wildly. I have only had one nightmare that I can remember and while I don't remember what it was about, I do remember the feeling I was left with when it was over.

Whatever the storyline in a nightmare, it always uncovers hidden issues about which you are holding fear. Nightmares tend to come to those believers who are too busy during the day to give God the quiet time it requires to hear Him clearly. Because you may not be giving God the time He needs, He brings you messages and instructions once you are asleep, when there are no distractions stopping you from hearing Him. Because Satan does not want you to hear from God, even in your sleep he uses nightmares to attempt to block what God is trying to communicate to you.

The most disturbing experience of nightmares I have ever heard happened to Chad, who was a high school senior when I was a junior at Timberline High School. We rode the same bus and as we waited for the bus in the mornings he always looked tired. One morning I asked him why he always looked so sleepy and he began to tell me that he had the same reoccurring nightmare over and over for weeks on end. I will never forget the name of the main character of his dream that used to chase him and threaten to kill him every night in his dream – Benoodle Sploowee.

While you may not have nightmares about an alter-ego named Benoodle Sploowee, I know that if you have been having nightmares, you are ready to get rid of them once and for all.

Apprehension

Dictionary.com defines apprehension as "anticipation of adversity or misfortune; suspicion or fear of future trouble or evil." When you have apprehension, you fear imagined danger and this feeling arises from the unclean fruit called apprehension.

Anxiety

A close relative to apprehension is anxiety. One major difference is that anxiety can be triggered by just about anything, even seemingly positive events. Anxiety can come from fear you are holding about anything, ranging from a first date to taking a test the next day in Algebra. It can be triggered by a memory, thoughts or being too busy. Anxiety is intensified worrying and is another manifestation of the spirit of fear.

Cowardice/Being Overly Cautious

Did you know that when we move in full faith of God, you live your life knowing that God will protect you and you cease to be overly careful or cautious? While this does not mean that you do not use wisdom, you do let go of always being on the lookout for things to go wrong.

Last week, I ordered an internet phone adapter to experiment with reducing my telephone costs. I was instant messaging with their live online customer service representative because they put a large hold on my debit card funds that I wanted them to release. In the process of the chat, their customer service representative asked me for my credit card number.

While I was not looking for them to do me wrong, it was not wise for me to provide my full debit card number, so I replied," No, I will not be providing you with my debit card number. That would not be wise for me to do." Using wisdom is different than being overly cautious or careful.

Being overly careful or cautious also shows up in parents who are overly protective of their children. It is rooted in the constant fear of something going wrong. If left untamed, it can turn into full-blow paranoia. As a result they barely allow their children to leave the house.

Growing up, I had a best friend named Charlotte, whose father was so overly protective, it almost destroyed her. He was so busy protecting her from the "mean" outside world that he never even realized that the real danger lurked inside of their house. In her father's fear of something bad happening to her, he always made Charlotte stay home with her older step brother. In the end, the step-brother repeatedly molested her.

The last time I talked to Charlotte, as a thirty-four year old adult, she was still carrying the profound pain of her childhood and was unable to break the generational curse. When she had a son, she became extremely overly cautious and careful with him and was doing the very same thing to her son. She wouldn't ever take her eyes off of him. She wanted to ensure that no one could get to him like her step-brother was allowed access to her as a result of her father's extreme caution. Being overly cautious does not allow others to have the life experiences that are required to mature and succeed in the world.

Intimidation/Fear of man

Another way to think of fear of man is to think of being intimidated by people. If there is someone who has a particular level of experience or title that intimidates you, then you are experiencing the fear of man.

Fear of man can also show up when you put someone on a pedestal. We are all human beings and striving for the same things as believers. No one is superior to anyone else, no matter the title or position in the church or the world. Yes, you still show honor and respect, but you are not to be intimidated by anyone else no matter how much experience they have in a certain arena, what business they own, how much money they have, or how long they have been in ministry.

Worry

While the Word clearly instructs us not to worry (Matthew 6:25 – 34), many of us spend an inordinate amount of time worrying about things you can begin to think that it is to be expected if you have a pulse. Worry is a result of not trusting God and fearing that things are going to end up a negative way.

Living worry-free no matter what is going on around you, is one of the greatest challenges you may face. I remember years ago when God first began to teach me how to stop worrying about the financial ups and downs of living on faith and trusting Him for the provision of me and my daughter.

About five years ago, my 1995 Chevy Blazer needed new tires. Okay, let me tell the truth – I was in dire need of some new tires and I did not have the money for them at the time. I was so worried about the tires on my car blowing out from the wear and tear on them. I worried so bad, that I could not even drive around the corner to the grocery store without my shoulders being in a knot from worrying.

Then, one day as I was praying, God asked me if I would believe that He would provide for me. I immediately thought of my worn-out tires. He reminded me that I am to trust him no matter what. I realized that if He is the God that He says He is, He knew exactly when I needed new tires and would provide the money for them at that time.

I let go of all the worry. I decided that God would protect me and provide for new tires. I drove knowing that I would know when I needed new tires because the money would appear. I made a faith move and took my car in for an estimate for four new tires so I would know what amount to ask God for - $483.

Less than a week later, I went to my mailbox and there was an unexpected and anonymous check for $500, more than enough for me to get the tires. There was a letter in the envelope with the check that read that this was a gift and I was not to share with anyone that I had received it. I was just supposed to use the money on whatever I wanted to. I made it to *Discount Tires* with no problems at all to get my new set of tires.

Shyness/Timidity

I know that you probably took a double-take to make sure you were reading this correctly. Yes, shyness and timidity are the fruits of unclean spirits and not personality traits. Even though you may be thinking that you have been that way all of your life, it is just the result of an unclean spirit that has been passed down to you through your family line.

While you may be more introverted than someone else, introverts can still function, speak and have regular eye contact. Shyness and timidity is something different. There is usually a powerful and self-expressed person trapped inside of a shy or timid person just wanting to come out, but having a hard time finding its way out. That is because the real person is oppressed by an unclean spirit.

Inadequacy

If you often feel like you don't measure up to your own standards or the standards that you perceive others place on you, then you are dealing with this fruit. These feelings of inadequacy can be repaired once fear is cast out and by daily and focused renewing of your mind.

If you are plagued with rampant feelings of inadequacy where no person, no thing, no words or no amount of attention helps you feel worthy and adequate, you are dealing with a deeper level of self-rejection. This usually results from experiencing sexual violation. I will go into more detail on this when I teach on perverse spirit.

Tension/Stress

Contrary to popular belief, tension and stress are not part of the experience of being human. You are not supposed to have frequent occurrences of stress and tension in your life. Even as I moved forward in doing God's ministry full-time, I used to be stressed out and full of tension all the time. Why? For the simple reason that I had not gotten to a place where I completely trusted God.

I still stressed about cash flow, paying bills, getting everything done and all of the daily responsibilities of being the head of a ministry. As I continued to renew my mind and

Continuing to renew my mind.

understand how to move in the realm of the impossible, the stress and tension disappeared.

Now, I am so stress and tension free that sometimes I just laugh at myself. No matter what it looks like with my natural eyes, I no longer stress about things anymore. As long as I am moving in righteousness all the while continuing to grow in The Lord and do what I am called to do, everything else seems to have a way of being taken care by God and His favor. This place of trust is where Jesus needs you to be.

Fear of Poverty

When I was in college at Howard University in Washington DC, I had a vision of a weekend conference that brought together men and women to heal the pain that we have experienced. I met a male counterpart from California, who lectured around the country. We had the same vision to bring men and women together to create strategic partnerships to impact their communities. We spent hours on the phone planning a conference where he would work with the men and I would work with the women. Then, at the end of the weekend we would bring them together to share their transformation.

I decided to spend the summer before my senior year in California so we could launch the conferences. I clearly recall the first meeting we had. The moment I set foot in his house, I was struck by the huge containers of everything that he had. It was like he went to a wholesale warehouse and went buck wild.

He didn't just have extra paper towels, he had about two or three dozen paper towels lined up on top of his kitchen cabinets. I stood in his kitchen and took it all in. Not only did he have paper towels, but he had everything in massive amounts - animal crackers, napkins, dishwashing detergent, cereal, chili, and spices. I thought to myself, "Okaaaay".

It wasn't until I went to use his restroom that I really knew that this man was dealing with some real issues. He had an entire drawer of soap (I just *had* to look), a cabinet full of toilet tissue, shaving lotion, and toothpaste. And he lived alone!

I remember standing in his bathroom thinking, "This didn't come up in our conversations. How am I going to approach this one?" I figured either he had a serious conspiracy theory going on and was imagining that one day soon he was going to be barricaded in his house and others would be coming in large numbers to seek refuge or he had a severe fear of poverty. Thank goodness it was the latter.

When I asked him about why he had such extreme amounts of goods stored up, he shared with me that he grew up poor and had promised himself at a young age that he would not live that way. It did not end with dry goods, his fear of poverty was evident in every area of his life.

He did not spend a penny on his surroundings and I could barely tell whether I was in a duplex straight from 1972 or the mid-1990's. It still had the same pewky-brownish shag carpet and wall paper. He had no pictures up or anything else that would have required a monetary investment in his environment.

I guess I should have known that our business arrangement wouldn't work when he showed up the first night in a car that was so "economical" that my legs barely fit in it. It looked like a roller skate. He did not even want to invest in a radio for the car. This was the first time that I literally saw what a car that had absolutely no embellishments and was rolled straight off of the assembly line actually looked like.

If that clue me in, when he picked me up for our second meeting, he still had on the same shorts he must have worn in high school (you remember those short-shorts with the big, white trim around the seam), knee socks and a Members-only jacket. I hadn't seen any of those pieces of clothes since the seventies! I don't mean the fashion that has come back around, these were the original pieces.

It was his fear of poverty that kept him bound and unable to really enjoy his present life. He hoarded things in bulk in fear that he would one day run out and not have enough. While this is an extreme case, it is one of the ways that fear of poverty can manifests itself.

Phobias

Phobias consist of any fears you have of things in the natural world. Spiders, heights, small spaces, etc.). I know that there are entire psychological practices centered on studying and helping people live with phobias. The Truth is that phobias are fruits of unclean spirits. When you fully understand that there is no fear in God, you will feel safe even in the midst of potential phobias.

Nervousness

Nervousness goes right along with stress, tension , worry, and anxiety. Whether you experience "butterflies" before speaking publicly, taking a test, or when you are nervous about anything, it is a result of an unclean spirit . Therefore, it can be removed from your life. Even if your Aunt Mary said that she just had "bad nerves," she was just experiencing this manifestation of the spirit of fear.

Overanalyzing

Are you someone who "thinks something to death?" If you overanalyze and over think things before you take a single action, then you are an over analyzer. I call it "analysis paralysis." It occurs when you think about things so hard in your head that you literally talk yourself out of taking action or the possibility of it succeeding.

You keep gathering more details, facts, and information to the point of overwhelm. Then you feel so buried that you do not know how to get from under your own thoughts. This is a form of the spirit of fear and is designed to keep you thinking so hard about something that you never actually take action to make your goals happen. Therefore, the instruction of God will not be able to manifest in your life.

While the spirit of fear is the stronghold that we talk about the most in the church, there are more that have taken hold of your life and are hindering you from walking in God's calling on your life. You need to understand each of them and how they manifest in order to be free from not just fear, but *all* unclean stronghold spirits. Let's talk about the spirit of bondage, as it also has most believers in its grips.

SPIRIT OF BONDAGE

The spirit of bondage is a stronghold spirit that is also extremely prevalent in the Body of Christ today. There may be so many aspects of your life that feel like they are in bondage that it can be hard to distinguish. You may refer to them as things that are keeping you "feeling stuck." While all unclean spirits keep you feeling bound, the spirit of bondage has some unique attributes that you must understand so you know which fruit is from bondage and which is from other strongholds.

When I first become acquainted with someone's life God has sent me to be a vessel for cleaning, I most often hear them trying to describe this stronghold by saying something like, "No matter what I do and how hard I try, it just seems like I can't get ahead." Or, "I feel like I am just going through the motions in my life and nothing is really making a real difference."

I often use the description of "that treadmill feeling" in their lives. They are doing everything their church or the world is telling them to move forward, yet they feel like they really aren't getting anywhere.

Other signs that you are dealing with the spirit of bondage include feeling like you have been stuck in the same place for years. If you look back on your life over the last three years and do not have much evidence of moving forward or manifesting anything that impacts others, you are dealing with the spirit of bondage. If you literally feel like something has you tied up and you just can't see it, that is the spirit of bondage.

I can just hear you wondering, "But Ericka, can't it be that it just hasn't been my due season?" You are always in a season. When you hear "due season" it means your harvest season - that season where you can harvest all that you have been planting and nurturing in your life. No matter what season you are in, you should always be moving forward. Even if you are in a drought or dry season, you should be learning new revelation and taking action daily. When you are experiencing the spirit of bondage, it feels different because you can barely move, no matter how hard you try.

The Fruit of The Spirit of Bondage

- ☐ Anguish
- ☑ Bitterness
- ☐ Satanic Captivity
- ☐ Blindness
- ☑ Being Shattered or Broken
- ☑ Lack of clarity of vision *of God's will*
- ☐ Addictions
- ☐ Greed
- ☐ Lust
- ☐ Compulsory sin
- ☐ "Submission" to the point of losing Self
- ☐ Legalism
- ☐ Chronic lack of time
- ☐ Overwhelm
- ☐ Over or Underweight

How the Spirit of Bondage Enters

The spirit of bondage enters like most strongholds enter, through sin and inequity. This unclean spirit often gets passed down through generations of families, which makes it difficult to track exactly when it entered your life.

Anguish

Have you ever met someone who seems like they almost enjoy suffering? No matter what good news you may share with them, they have a "woe is me and watch-out-the-world-is-out-to-get-me" mentality. They seem to be literally in mental, emotional and physical agony constantly and almost seem to have no interest in living any differently. They seem to almost make up reasons to be distressed even when there may not be a good reason to do so. Then, you have encountered someone who is anguished.

Bitterness

At some point in their lives, most people have experienced some sort of emotional hurt or pain, but someone living with bitterness does not know how to let it go. They have deep animosity and are spiteful toward others. What began as deep emotional pain or trauma has hardened into toxicity and the inability to forgive others and themselves. The longer bitterness is allowed to exist, the more it hardens your heart and creates a nearly invincible guard around you.

Joy, peace, kindness, gentleness, patience and love cannot co-exist with someone who is living with the fruit of bitterness in their lives. It makes authentic joy and even smiling difficult. People experiencing bitterness can be draining to be around because nothing seems to cheer them up. They seem to "suck" all of the air out of a room.

Satanic Captivity

While all unclean spirits are a form of satanic captivity, this fruit is more extreme. As I write each of these descriptions, the Holy Spirit shows me specific examples. Immediately, I saw an image of someone dressed in "Goth." That is the term my teenage daughter uses to describe someone who is constantly dressing in black, listening to destructive music, obsessively piercing their body, rebels against everything and anything they can, and usually wears images of skulls and skeletons anywhere they can on their body. Violent images of death often accompany someone experiencing satanic captivity.

Satanic captivity can also show up through cutting yourself and terrorizing people around you. When you delve into the world of darkness and want to stay there, it is a result of satanic captivity's direct and obvious hold on you. Other manifestations of satanic captivity include gangs and criminal lifestyles.

When I had been in Raleigh for about a year, one day I stopped to get gas at a nearby convenience store. My inner discernment was going off as a man approached me while I was standing at the gas pump. He asked me for some change.

I stopped and really looked at him. He could not look me in the eye and I could feel a satanic spirit about him. I knew better than to go in my car to get any change at that point so I told him that I had something better than spare change – I would pray for God to move him out of his struggle.

He thanked me and shared that he gave up on God a long time ago. He even shared that he had given his life over the to the devil years ago. I knew that he was experiencing satanic captivity. When you have repeatedly defiled your temple, you make an unspoken pact that you are open to satanic influence. It is literally agreeing with the devil that you will do his work and live his way.

Blindness

When you are dealing with bondage, you are unable to see things in the spirit realm clearly. You are also unable to see your vision or the things you should be doing to further God's calling clearly. It seems like you are trying to see through a fog. You cannot recognize the things of Christ.

When I am teaching or preaching, I always begin with a prayer that asks God to open up the ears and eyes of all those who are there. Your eyes can become covered from the things of God.

If this goes unchecked, it can manifest in physical blindness. (Matthew 4:16; John 1:4; John 3:19)

Your spiritual eyes should be seeing more and more everyday. Jesus often healed blindness in the Bible and that same healing is available for our spiritual and physical blindness today.

Being Shattered or Broken

Have you ever seen someone who has been emotionally shattered? They can no longer keep the pieces together and have just fallen apart. When someone is shattered or deeply wounded, it does not matter how long ago they experienced the trauma. It feels like it was just yesterday for them and they cannot seem to recover, no matter how hard they try.

> *A man's spirit sustains him in sickness, but a crushed spirit who can bear? – Proverbs 18:14*

In Mary Garrison's book, *How To Try A Spirit*, she used the term "bruised." I shifted the term for clarity. Someone who is dealing with the fruit "shattered" has been through something that was so devastating to them that it left them crushed, bruised, and in pieces. Their heart and spirit have been broken so many times that it seems to have only slivers and shattered pieces left.

They have been through some sort of trauma that has left his or her life in shambles and they seem unable to pick up the pieces and put them back together. This is someone who has been shattered. It is not the process of being shattered itself that opens the door for this fruit, but the person's inability to move forward that has kept the door open. Feeling shattered often goes hand and hand with bitterness.

Lack of Clarity of Vision

One of my guiding values is clarity. I have learned that I operate best when I am what I call "crystal clear." This clarity always comes from the Holy Spirit and without the Holy Spirit, you are left trying to figure out things on your own. You know you are lacking clarity of vision when you are not certain what God has called you to do and what purpose He would have you fulfill.

I often hear people say, "I know I am supposed to help people, but I'm not sure beyond that." That is what people say when they have a lack of clarity of vision in their lives. This lack of clarity is caused by the spirit of bondage as it prevents you from seeing and hearing God clearly.

Addictions

All addictions are fruit of the spirit of bondage. An addiction is something on which you become dependent and your body craves it until you satisfy it with the addiction. You are addicted when you habitually or compulsively give yourself over to something that is getting in the way of your walk with God.

The list of substances one can be addicted to is long – cigarettes, alcohol, food, sugar, carbohydrates, drugs, sex, shopping, money – and on and on. As long as you are involved in addiction, you are controlled and are locked out of all God has for you.

Greed

Greed is defined by Webster as, "The excessive desire, especially for food or wealth." Greed creates an insatiable appetite for material possessions and power. Greed in the area of food is what we call gluttony. The overindulgence goes far beyond what any one person needs to be emotionally and physically healthy and is an expression of a stronghold on your life.

Greed shows up in many of the children of this generation. They are so bombarded with images of what they just *have* to have that they develop an insatiable longing for more and more. They may have an mp3 player and want an IPod. They may have a cell phone that works perfectly fine and want a Smartphone that can surf the web in record time. You name it - shoes, clothes, electronics, music downloads, play stations, Wii games, money, etc. They just can't seem to get enough.

Greedy people often brag and have a difficult time sharing their possessions with others, unless it is for wanting false admiration from others.

When greed goes unchecked in your life, you bring it with you right into adulthood. For women, greed can show up when you never have enough shoes or clothes. It often shows up in pairs of tennis shoes, electronic gadgets, or cars for men. Whatever the form of greed, it has you bound to the very thing with which you are being greedy.

Lust

Lust goes hand-in-hand with greed in that you crave things that feed or temporarily satisfy your flesh. We tend to think of lust only in the context of sexual appetite, but it goes far beyond lusting for the flesh of another person. You are lusting after someone or something when you desire it passionately and longingly. You often fantasize about the things you lust for. Lust is not a "normal" part of life, but it is a form of bondage.

I can spot lust a mile away. There is a certain look someone gets in their eyes when they are lusting. They don't even have to say anything. I am particularly keen at spotting sexual desire and lust from men. It does not always mean that they are going to take action on their lust, they simply just look at a woman lustfully. Women often do the same thing toward men.

It is as prevalent in the church as it is at a downtown bar. It is as prevalent from a long-standing church member as it is from someone just coming to church for the first time in years. Lust does not care who it manifests in. It will use a saved person just as much as an unsaved person. You must be delivered from the bondage of lust so it disappears from your life.

Compulsory sin

As I was nearing the explanation for this fruit, I could not have written it even a day sooner. Prior to today, I had never experienced someone with this fruit manifest in their life and I would have had a difficult time putting it into words. But, I was up late last night watching a movie that so perfectly demonstrated compulsory sin.

Someone dealing with compulsory sin actually finds sinning irresistible because they are filled with darkness and darkness is drawn to darkness. They keep sinning knowing what they are doing is wrong and that there is a consequence for it. They gain some sort of twisted sense of power and satisfaction from their actions.

Last night I veered from my normal corny film pattern and watched a movie set in Sixteenth century England. It was about two wealthy aristocrats who had nothing better to do than to plot the desecration and destruction of those who appeared to love God.

The male character in the movie actually gained great pleasure from "conquering" the most devout and pious women he could find. He had a sinister laugh when he thought of the power he seemed to gain when he seduced a woman of God.

I am always amazed at just how deliberately evil people can be. This was a great example of compulsory sin and how it takes a hold on you and refuses to let go.

Spirit of stupor

The first time I heard the Word, "stupor," I was playing a part in the high school play, *Little Abner,* that was performed my sophomore year at Timberline High School. I had a small part in the play and after so many rehearsals I began to learn the lines and cues of the other actors. One of the scenes was a group song and dance in which little Abner was coming out of a stupor.

I have to admit, I thought it was some word used only in the back woods of small towns, until I saw it in the Bible

> *...as it is written: "God gave them a spirit of stupor, eyes so that they could not see and ears so that they could not hear, to this very day." – Romans 11:8*

This spirit causes you to be spiritually blind and deaf to the Truth of God. It could also be listed with Deaf and Dumb spirit as it covers your ears from hearing the things of God.

"Submission" to the point of losing Self

This one was not even on the list until I recently experienced it and asked the Holy Spirit which unclean fruit was in operation. Then, I began to recognize this dynamic over and over again with Christian women in their marriages.

This form of bondage comes into play when one spouse, most often the woman, loses their identity in the marriage. This is a tricky place to walk because I truly believe in the power of submission but this goes beyond submission to bondage. The church has truly misunderstood submission.

True submission honors who you are, it does not cause you to lose who you are. When the Word teaches that wives are to submit to their husbands, the teaching often ends there. That scripture also says that husbands should love their wives like Jesus loved the Church and Jesus gave His very life for the love of the Church. Yet I witness far too many wives giving up their vision and identity for their husbands and the husbands not honoring them as it instructs in the Word.

> *Wives, submit to your husbands as to the Lord. For the husband is the head of the wife as Christ is the*

> *head of the church, his body, of which he is the Savior. Now as the church submits to Christ, so also wives should submit to their husbands in everything.*

Here is the part I seldom hear people referring to when they talk about this scripture.

> *Husbands, love your wives, just as Christ loved the church and gave himself up for her to make her holy, cleansing her by the washing with water through the Word, and to present her to himself as a radiant church, without stain or wrinkle or any other blemish, but holy and blameless.*
>
> *In this same way, husbands ought to love their wives as their own bodies. He who loves his wife loves himself. After all, no one ever hated his own body, but he feeds and cares for it, just as Christ does the church— for we are members of his body. "For this reason a man will leave his father and mother and be united to his wife, and the two will become one flesh.– Ephesians 5:22 - 31*

When you become so bound by the life of your spouse that you lose your ability to hear God and act on what God is telling you, it is a form of bondage. When your spouse is not honoring the Word of God in the way he or she treats you, it is a form of bondage and cannot be allowed to persist.

Legalism

Anytime the Word of God is taken out of context and leaves no space to enjoy your life due to man's rules and regulations, it is legalism. When the fruits of the Holy Spirit are not present, it ceases to be of God. Legalism is the excessive adherence to laws, rules, or a way of living based on man's judgment. It is the Holy Spirit's role to cleanse and purge you of past sins, behaviors and vices. This is not the role of a man.

When we become judgmental and so narrowly focused in the church, your devotion turns to man away from God and becomes legalism. This is an unclean spirit and actually keeps you from experiencing the freedom and liberty Jesus promises.

Legalistic religions and affiliations are so rigid that people usually end up calling them cults or overly ritualistic religious systems. When the teaching of any church or organization becomes so rigid that it begins to teach that you are to not interact with others within or outside of the Body of Christ, you know you are heading toward legalism. You can even see this in churches if you have been taught not to interact with those who have left that particular church. Jesus often interacted with unsaved people so he could spread his gospel and save the lost sheep.

Chronic lack of time

Have you ever met someone who rushes around all the time seems so busy that they are never available? Perhaps you feel like there is never enough time and you are being pulled in a thousand different directions. Yet, even with all you are doing, nothing seems to get done thoroughly. You are experiencing a chronic lack of time that God did not design your body to withstand.

While being overly busy can be a fruit of the spirit of fear because it is a form of hiding from the Truth. Chronic lack of time takes it to a new level. It is a form of bondage.

Overwhelm

You know you are overwhelmed when you feel like you have so much going on you that it feels like the walls of your life are closing in on you. Oxford dictionary actually says that one of the definitions of overwhelm is, "To be buried or drowned beneath a huge mass or to be overpowered with an excess of business." While being overwhelmed feels like a physical mass sitting on top of you, it is most often a feeling based on how you interact with responsibility and the pressures of your vision. It becomes unclean because when you are overwhelmed, you often stop looking to God and try to dig your way out. It keeps you unable to be grateful and experience the power of Jesus.

Over or Underweight

I was surprised to hear the Holy Spirit share with me that weight problems are a fruit of the spirit of bondage. I assumed that were a result of the spirit of heaviness or infirmity. One evening I was sitting on my bed thinking about my weight release program. I began to wonder what spirit I should be casting out so I asked the Holy Spirit.

I heard, "You are bound by the excess fat you are carrying on your body." I knew as soon as I heard the word "bound" that it was the spirit of bondage. Shortly after that, Jesus was doing deliverance through me with a young lady who was not eating. I also knew that this was the spirit of bondage keeping her bound and not eating enough food to properly nourish and strengthen her body. When your weight gets in the way of you moving in full obedience to God, it is an unclean fruit and Satan uses it to control you through your flesh.

SPIRIT OF HEAVINESS

The spirit of heaviness is easy to identify because it literally feels "heavy" for people who are oppressed with it. I was just speaking to Tonya, a friend I hadn't spoken to in almost twenty years, who called me today. We both attended New Life Baptist Church when we were younger.

As she was updating me on her life, she shared how she had to distance herself from one of the girls she grew up with at New Life. She shared that her friend's energy was just feeling too heavy and sucking the life out of her. Her description perfectly captured what it feels like when you experience someone oppressed with the spirit of heaviness.

The other way I often describe the spirit of heaviness is that it feels like you are trying to move through quicksand or with cement blocks attached to your ankles. It takes ten times the energy to even wake up and get out of bed in the morning when you are oppressed with heaviness. You become exhausted easily and as a result, your energy is usually low. You then have to leech the energy of others, without even being aware of it.

The Fruit of the Spirit of Heaviness

- ❏ Mourning
- ❏ Grief
- ❏ Sadness
- ❏ Sorrow
- ☑ Depression
- ❏ Whining
- ❏ Extreme emotions
- ❏ Hopelessness
- ❏ Loneliness
- ❏ Discouragement

☐ Rejection
☐ Self-pity
☐ Gloominess
☐ Extreme and constant negativity
☐ Crying Easily/Constantly on the verge of tears
☐ Laziness
☐ Gluttony

How the Spirit of Heaviness Enters

The spirit of heaviness usually enters through the door of unhealed emotional issues as a child or young adult. It also can be a generational spirit if one or both of your parents lived with an unhealed heart.

It can also enter into adults through the loss of a loved one with whom things were not complete or fully communicated before they passed away. Again, it is not as important to know how the unclean spirit got in, as it is imperative to get it out and learn the steps to emotional healing so you prevent the heaviness from ever re-entering your temple or family again.

Mourning

When you lose a loved one who was very dear to you, there is a natural mourning process. You can also mourn the loss of a relationship or something dear to you in your life. Perhaps your family was required to move from a city that you really enjoyed, or you have to move on from a church that has become your family. As God moves you forward in His vision, part of the natural course of action is for Him to require you to separate yourself from certain people, circumstances and situations along the way.

The natural process of mourning gets better with each day that passes as you learn a new rhythm of living without that person in your day-to-day life. When this deep sorrow or regret becomes prolonged over years and does not seem to be getting better every day, it is evidence that it is an unclean spirit that has found a way into your life and heart.

Grief

Grief goes hand-in-hand with the symptoms of mourning. While you can be expected to grieve the loss of someone or something in your life, it should subside as you create new ways to remember and honor the life of your loved one. While you will always miss the presence of your loved one, grief should not last so long that it keeps you tied to the loss and never allows you to get to a place of gratitude for the time you shared with that person. If grief is allowed to remain, it actually causes undue suffering and misery.

I recently lost my Mama Doris, a dear friend of the family who grew up like a sister to my mother. Her family became my extended family. Mama Doris attended a primitive Baptist church in Mobile, Alabama, where they had a prolonged time to grieve the loss of a member.

When at church, my Papa Leon, her husband, is required to sit next to a piece of black lace draped over the seat Mama Doris occupied. This black lace is required to stay for several months following her passing. I always wondered if that tradition allowed Papa Leon to actually move on from her loss or exasperated his grief.

It is possible to lose a loved one and feel joy, peace, and love throughout the process. I have been to home going services where people are laughing and remembering the wonderful life and memories they had with the person who passed on.

Sadness

Some of the words used to describe sadness are melancholy, downcast, dejected, morose, blue, brokenhearted, gloomy and miserable. These words do a great job of further describing when the emotion of sadness becomes prolonged and can actually become a fruit of heaviness.

While sadness is a normal emotion to occasionally experience, the sadness that manifests when it is the spirit of heaviness is a deep sadness that feels like it is dragging you deeper and deeper into it everyday. When this occurs, you can't seem to shake the sadness no matter how hard you try. When this sadness is allowed to remain and grow, it actually turns into sorrow or prolonged sadness.

Sorrow

When sadness becomes prolonged, it turns into sorrow and feels like you are at the bottom of a deep pit, looking up at the daylight. Sorrow feels like you can wail and moan because you are in such a deep place of emotional pain and affliction.

People who are experiencing sorrow always have something negative to share, no matter how positive and wonderful an experience may be. It reminds me of the little cartoon character from *Gulliver's Travels* cartoon that used to come on in the seventies, who was always saying, "We'll never make it" in his deep, raspy and sorrowful voice.

Depression

When sorrow is allowed to exist in a person's life, it can grow into depression. There is no medication to truly cure depression because it is a spiritual issue. I often see a commercial for a drug used to "treat" depression give the statistic that more than ninety percent of people on medication for depression still experience the symptoms of depression. Something is terribly wrong with that picture.

I actually developed a theory when I began coaching clients who were diagnosed with depression and on medication. I believe that depression is the space between living your calling and just existing. I have worked with many clients that were no longer depressed and fully came off of their medication once we got their lives aligned with who God created them to be and not the one they had been living, which allowed the space for depression to come in.

Before I made the decision to live God's vision for my life, I experienced depression. The only way I can describe it is that I felt like I was at the bottom of a huge, deep hole and dirt was being poured on top of me everyday. I felt helpless and did not have the energy or motivation to do the very things that would ward off the depression.

I just thought I was "out of sorts" and did not realize I was experiencing depression, until I read an *Ebony* magazine article that described each and every symptom of depression. I was experiencing all of them. I knew that it was a result of existing in a life that was nowhere near what I really wanted and desired. When I looked at my life, it did not even resemble the life I knew I was born to live. I put myself on a program I called, "Project Humpty Dumpty" because I was in pieces and it was time to put myself back together again.

After months on my self-prescribed "Project Humpty Dumpty" program, I was able to climb out of the hole of depression. I wish I knew then what I know now, because I would have understood what was really going on and how to remove it from my life in an instant.

Whining

Have you ever met an adult who whines profusely? I always notice this because I am truly allergic to whining from children – including my own – not to mention in adults. It feels like the equivalent of someone running their fingernails across a chalkboard to me.

I have two uncles that whine – literally. When they talk to me, they always use long, drawn out words with a higher tone of voice. I was relieved to find out that this was a manifestation of heaviness and that they were not natural whiners and complainers. To this day when my daughter attempts to whine, I say, "Use your mature voice or you won't get a response from me." She straightens up quickly. Somehow, I haven't felt comfortable saying this to my uncles.

Extreme emotions

Do you know someone who is up one minute and down the next? Or they can explode without a moment's notice? This is someone who is living with this fruit of the spirit of heaviness. The world may call them "bipolar" or "moody." They exist on a roller coaster of emotions and you never know which mood they are in or what sets off their moods.

I had a friend that kept me on eggshells around her for years. I never knew what I would say that would set her off and make her cuss at me and abruptly hang up the phone. I tolerated it for years because she was a dear friend of mine and when she was "up" she was delightful.

Luckily, God allowed me to be a vessel for her deliverance and she is free from this manifestation. Now, she is steady, consistent, and amazed at how mellow she now feels even when things that used to set her off occur.

It is not just "that time of the month" or a "mood swing" that causes these extreme emotions. It is a tool that Satan uses to keep you from moving forward in who you are in God. You were created to be consistent and unshakeable by the things in the natural world. If you are undergoing anything other than emotional steadiness and consistency, it is a sign that this fruit has been growing in your life.

Hopelessness

Hope is knowing that no matter what your life looks like, God has something better for you. It is being certain that things are getting better and that the challenges you are experiencing are only temporary. Hope gives you the ability to believe that a brighter day is on the way. Hope is the prerequisite for belief and faith. Hope is what gives you the strength to wait on the Lord's promises for your life (Psalm 130:5).

Living with hopelessness is not a personality trait. It is an unclean spirit. You are experiencing hopelessness when you feel like you no longer have any options and you don't seem able to remain hopeful as hard as you may try.

Loneliness

There is a word we use to describe perpetually lonely people – "loner." We justify their loneliness by saying, "Oh, little Johnny or Suzy has always been a loner. That is just how he is." No. This is not true. While it may be all you know of him or her, it is due to the oppression of the spirit of heaviness. When you are surrounded by people and still feel lonely, you know that you are dealing with the unclean fruit loneliness.

Loneliness is different than the spiritual isolation God requires of you when He sets you apart from other believers and the world. Loneliness is a deep emotional state of perpetually feeling alone, no matter how many people may be around you at any given time.

Discouragement

Each of these manifestations of heaviness are becoming quite obvious, right? Discouragement robs you of your confidence and courage to do the things that will move you forward. When you are discouraged you feel disheartened and have a difficult time feeling encouraged. When you are dealing with discouragement, you easily take things personally and often interpret people's reaction toward you and your actions as critical or unsupportive.

Rejection

While fear of rejection is a form of the spirit of fear, rejection always leaves you feeling not good enough and like you are unworthy of being noticed. Instead of just accepting that God has something else that will serve you better, you take things very personally and assume that you deserved to be discarded or passed up for an opportunity or relationship.

I heard a new term from Catherine, a sister in Christ of mine at my former church – "asker." She shared that your "asker" is the internal mechanism that guides you in asking for help or contribution from others. You may have a broken "asker."

I often work with clients in helping them learn how to ask for help or what they really want or need from others. They have to literally fix their "asker" and learn how to be clear about what they need and then be able to feel safe in asking for it. If you are feeling rejected, your "asker" may need repairing.

Self-pity

In keeping with the theme of the fruits of the spirit of heaviness, self-pity also can manifest. You know you have crossed into self-pity when you are feeling extreme sorrow for your perceived troubles.

You know you are in the presence of someone who is stuck in self-pity because he or she has a way of turning any issue inward on him or herself. No matter what you are sharing with that person, he or she always seem to turn the discussion back to feeling sorry for him or herself, trying to get you to feel sorry for them. While you may have been thinking that this was just part of what makes that person who he or she is, it is indeed another demonstration of the spirit of heaviness.

Gloominess

I became intimately familiar with gloominess while growing up in Washington State. The weather is grey and overcast for most of the year and the word we use to describe it is "gloomy." It perfectly describes the clouds that hover in the sky and surround you with a fogginess that you just can't seem to shake.

Those living with gloominess seem to be surrounded by invisible overcast skies and grey clouds all of the time. Gloominess reminds me of the *Peanuts* cartoon character, Pigpen, with his very own little cloud of stinky dust that lingers around him at all times. No matter where someone dealing with gloominess goes or whatever they do, that little cloud always remains nearby.

Extreme and constant negativity

You can say, "I am so excited about my new business."

They will reply, "You know ninety-five percent of all businesses fail in the first year, right?"

You may say, "I met a wonderful man that I really like and connected with."

They can respond by saying, "Yeah, my last boyfriend seemed wonderful and he turned out to be the worst decision of my life."

You can say, "I won the lottery."

They will say, "I watched this documentary about how all lottery winners end up broke all over again."

You want to ask," Can you be positive about anything?"

While the conversation may be different with this unclean fruit, you will always be left asking yourself if that person can be positive or happy about anything. The answer is no.

As bad as they may want to, depending on the degree of oppression, they will not be able to bring positivity out of their mouths until they are fully delivered from their constant negativity. No one likes being the" party-poop" and would not be if they understood how it affects others and how to avoid it.

Crying Easily/Constantly on the verge of tears

Long before I was delivered from this stronghold, I used to be able to cry at the drop of a hat. I have even been known to cry during a touching commercial. I remember going to a Disney movie with my daughter and she kept leaning over in disbelief that I was crying. I felt like I was always on the verge of tears for one reason or another.

It did not take much to set off my tears. After a conversation with someone that upset me, I could keep it together while I was talking to that person, but the moment I hung up the phone or left his or her presence, I was in a crying heap on the nearest pillow. I spent years trying to develop the skills to hide it.

I was incredibly relieved to find out that I could live without this feeling and you can also be free from it for good.

Laziness

Before I do a coaching session, I usually have the client answer a quick homework assignment that includes asking them to identify their biggest time-wasters and excuses. They often answer that question by saying that they have been lazy.

After a few short questions, I can uncover that it is not laziness they are fighting but being overloaded. True laziness is a profound sluggishness that feels inescapable. You actually lose your desire to do almost anything and the most appealing place can easily become the couch, with the nearest remote control in your hand.

If you are carrying laziness, you know you should be doing something more, you just can't bring yourself to move or take action. It feels like something is sitting on top of your dreams and you don't have the energy to fight it. Thus, you just let it slowly drag you under until you stop trying to tread the waters of your life. Lazy people know better, but they just can't respond to what they know to do.

Gluttony

There is the enjoyment of food and coming together with friends and family around a good meal. Then, there is eating to stuff down emotions and how you really feel. You know you have crossed over into gluttony when you turn to food for reasons other than sustenance of your body and can't seem to stop.

When you develop an insatiable appetite and move into excess eating, you are demonstrating the power of the unclean fruit named 'gluttony.'

Have you noticed that you never seem to overdo it on fruits and vegetables? It is always the sweets and "comfort" foods that you overindulge in. When you become a glutton for food, you have a difficult time stopping short of engorging yourself; yet you know what you are doing is actually harming you. The term "glutton for punishment," actually derived from this concept.

Okay, that summarizes the fruit of the spirit of heaviness. If you were like me when you read this, I was checking off almost everything on the list. Isn't it great to know that you don't have to live with this spirit sitting on top of your life?

SPIRIT OF WHOREDOMS

I always warn people who have opened the door to the spirit of whoredoms because it sounds so harsh. Spirit of whoredoms enters when you do not feel loved and attempt to replace things to try to fill the hole that only love can fill.

In scripture, the word "whoredoms" identifies those who replace the love of God with other idols and foul behavior. It is used in the spirit for those who turned away from God and chose wickedness over serving God (Hosea 4:12 and 5:4). No one wants to admit that they have the spirit of whoredoms in their temple. But if you experienced not feeling loved as a child, chances are that this spirit has taken up residence in your life.

It manifests in the lives of people looking for love and admiration in inappropriate ways and are not intentionally trying to be wicked. It manifests very dangerously because it usually results in what the Word calls sinning against your own body.

> *Flee from sexual immorality. All other sins a man commits are outside his body, but he who sins sexually sins against his own body. – 1 Corinthians 6:18*

This is not about feeling guilty or making others who have been living with this spirit feel less loved by God. Remember, ninety-eight percent of the Body of Christ is dealing with countless manifestations of these spirits and they are all a result of a lack of understanding of the spiritual realm. This unclean spirit is not any worse than the others, although the symptoms of this unclean spirit take more of a toll on your body than the other spirits with the exception of dumb and deaf spirits, spirit of infirmity and perverse spirit (more on those later).

The Fruit of the Spirit of Whoredoms

- ☐ Inferiority/Rejection
- ☐ Guilt
- ☐ Shopaholic
- ☐ Promiscuity
- ☐ Under dressing/Inappropriate dressing
- ☐ Leaving God's covering/backsliding
- ☐ Harlotry/Prostitution
- ☐ Idolatry
- ☐ Love of the world
- ☐ Love of money
- ☐ Love of the body
- ☐ Adultery

How The Spirit of Whoredoms Enters

The spirit of whoredoms enters as a child when you do not feel loved. No matter how much your parents or guardians loved you, your perception was that you were not loved. If they did not show it in the language you needed to feel it, it opened the door for the spirit of whoredoms to enter into your life.

I have seen that this spirit is often generational and runs most frequently through the mother's family line as a result of her feeling unloved as a little girl. It also runs through the father's family line if he did not feel loved as a boy, often when the father was absent or preoccupied trying to earn a living and not spending quality time with his children.

Inferiority/Rejection

If you are someone dealing with this fruit of whoredoms, then you truly perceive that you are not good enough for the things that you desire. You are living with the assumption that you will be rejected, and therefore never attempt to go outside of your comfort zone. You easily talk yourself out of taking action on the premise that others are not going to accept you or your ideas.

This fruit appears in your life if you felt rejected as a child and not accepted from your parents or guardians. As you grew up, you attracted people and situations that actually reinforced your fear of rejection. This fear makes situations in which you have to present yourself to others for them to reach a decision about you, such as a job interview or dating situation, extremely challenging for you. No matter what happened in your past, you can live without these deep feelings of inferiority and rejection. It can also be linked to the spirit of fear.

Guilt

When you are carrying the spirit of whoredoms, guilt is usually not far behind. You may feel guilty about allowing anybody to do anything for you. You may feel guilty if anyone has to go out of their way on your behalf. This is part of the feelings of inadequacy and constantly feeling like you are not enough that this stronghold spirit creates.

Shopaholic

Yes, your eyes are focusing correctly; that does say, "shopaholic." Before you dismiss it or laugh, let me explain. When you feel a lack of love in your childhood, you find ways to attempt to fill the void that love should have filled. Far too often you may turn to material things to fill that void.

If you are a woman who has clothes in your closet with the tags still on them and cannot even remember exactly when you purchased them, it is a fruit of the spirit of whoredoms. If you are a man who loves to surround himself with electronic gadgets, cars, yard equipment, etc. then you are more than likely carrying this unclean spirit.

Anytime you attempt to fill the void of love with material possessions then you are under the oppression of this unclean fruit. You have moved past the point of purchasing items for use or to share with others to trying to find joy, happiness, and peace, which are never found in objects.

Promiscuity

When the spirit of whoredoms goes unchecked in the life of a child, it can turn into promiscuity when they become teenagers or young adults. This promiscuity can continue into adulthood if it is unrecognized and not properly addressed.

I intimately know this fruit because I lived with it for years as I searched for the love I was so deeply longing for through men. I was fine until my sophomore year in college and then I just went "buck wild." I had never experienced the interest or attention I was getting from men and I did not know how to handle it without having sex. Okay, that's another entire book, right? Whew!

Under dressing/Inappropriate dressing

Have you ever seen a woman or a young lady that was dressed too scantily and it did not even seem to faze her? I don't mean at the nightclub, I mean for work or for everyday attire. She was unknowingly carrying this fruit.

I will never forget the niece of one of my former boyfriends, who was only eight years old, she had the spirit of a "whore" about her. I remember seeing her one day at a church event and being blown away at the high heels, short skirt, and cut off tank top she had on. She had this sway in her hips that literally scared me. I was even more blown away that the family of my former boyfriend allowed her to go out in public dressed so inappropriately. It showed me that this spirit can enter even a child.

Even though someone will argue you down that he or she is dressing like he or she chooses, the truth is that the spirit of whoredoms within that person is drawn to those clothes. I remember writing in my first book that once you love yourself more and more, you cover up your body and realize that you are more than the skin you are in.

Leaving God's covering/backsliding

This fruit just goes to show how many tactics the enemy uses against us. Have you ever noticed that when people backslide that it is hard to come back to God? This is different than occasional sinning; this is literally being pulled toward dark behavior and habits.

It is a dangerous place to be because you are no longer under the covering of God, where you have access to His promises. But we serve such a merciful and graceful God. Once you sincerely confess and turn from the behavior that caused you to backslide, God welcomes you back into His loving arms.

Harlotry/Prostitution

As with all unclean fruit, this fruit gains more footing in your life the longer it is allowed to exist. When the spirit of whoredoms goes undiscovered it grows into you exchanging sex for money and using your flesh to manipulate others sexually. People engaged in this lifestyle justify their involvement as a way to survive or a means to an end, but in all honesty they are simply acting out this particular spirit.

Idolatry

Idolatry is the act of worshipping any other gods than Jesus. At a recent speaking engagement, I shared that I can always tell what idols are in people lives by the way they spend their time and what they think about the most.

There are many forms of idolatry. Anything that gets in the way of your focus on God has become an idol. The most common idol is people seeing their jobs, businesses and ministries as their source of provision instead of God. You may spend more time working, thinking about work, and preparing for work than you do about thinking about and preparing yourself for God.

For others, their idols may have become their significant others, their family, their business opportunity, the gym, fashion, or their friendships. Others may express idolatry by reading books by new age authors and spending more time in them than the Word. It may show up as watching television, movies or following the lives of celebrities. For others, the church or the pastor can become an idol if you see your pastor as the intercessor between you and God (this can only be the Holy Spirit). It is also idolatry when you replace the time you are to be focusing on communicating directly from God.

The Word talks of those who replace God for statues of wood, gold, and silver and those who replace the worship of God for the things that God created and not God Himself. Whatever the idol may be, it is creating a wedge from you knowing and hearing from God as you are designed to do.

Love of the world

The Word is very clear on its instruction as it relates to loving the world, or in other words, loving the things of the enemy.

> *Do not love the world or anything in the world. If anyone loves the world, the love of the Father is not in him. For everything in the world—the cravings of sinful man, the lust of his eyes and the boasting of what he has and does—comes not from the Father but from the world. – 2 John 2:15*

While we are designed to exist in the world, we are not to become part of the world and get too attached to the way the world does things. I am sure you have witnessed examples of what happens when Christians in your church get too attached to the world. It becomes a challenge to distinguish the believers from the world when you encounter them.

Love of money

Before I even elaborate on this unclean fruit, let me be clear that I fully believe that all people of God should be living His promise of life and life more abundantly (John 10:10). God is very clear that He puts all things under our feet and we are to be fruitful, multiply, and go and subdue all things in the earth (Gen 1:28). I do not believe that believers are to suffer financially as we need money to function effectively in the Kingdom.

We must always keep in mind that money is one of the tools God provided us and it is not ever to become our identity or something we love. Money is not evil; it is the love of money that is not of God. You are not to pursue and serve mammon, the god of money. You are to serve God and He will always present people the resources to carry out to His vision (Luke 6:38).

You know you are in love with money the moment it has the power to stress you out and make you worry. This is evidence that you have taken your eyes off of God and unknowingly shifted your focus to the pursuit of money.

I had to learn that God put money under my feet and that I am always to put ministering to people first. While we must put a value to our gifts from God so they can become our livelihood (1 Cor 9:14), never lose sight of the fact that it is God's wealth and simply a tool that opens up options. God desires to take you far beyond money, which man created.

Love of the body

When people first see this fruit on the list they often end up saying, "What?" to themselves. Allow me to elaborate. You know you have met someone who is under the spell of this fruit of the spirit of whoredoms when they are so into their bodies that there doesn't seem to be much else in their lives.

It most often shows up in men, but you can also witness it in women who seem obsessed with their bodies. I was watching a show on TV last night and it was showing the story of a woman who had undergone more than fifty plastic surgeries so she could look like *Barbie*. While it was not my place to judge her, it was evident to me what spirit was operating within her. She was obsessed with her body looking a certain way and she did not see any limits to what she would do to achieve the look she desired.

While it seldom manifests this powerfully in people, it certainly is evidence of something missing in their lives.

Adultery

Are you surprised to see this one listed under 'whoredoms?' While it could also be a result of perverse spirit, the truth is that when you seek love or sex outside of your marriage, you are trying to fill the same void created by a lack of feeling loved. You will try to fill that void, regardless of how many people you may hurt along the way. It is the spirit of whoredoms pulling you into this behavior as you attempt to put an adhesive bandage over the real issue that left you wounded in the first place.

You may either be relieved or concerned as you read through this list and see reflections of your life and the lives of those around you. I pray that you are recognizing fruit that has grown in your life and having huge "Aha!" moments in the process. Let's move on to the rest of the unclean spirits and their fruits, so you can get a full understanding of why you have been having the challenges you have been experiencing.

SPIRIT OF HAUGHTINESS

This is the spirit that governs pride, ego, and arrogance, and creates much of the division that the church is experiencing today. It has created the feeling that a church or congregation belongs to the pastor when in fact, the church and all who attend belong to Jesus.

The spirit of haughtiness is running rampant in the American church right now. This foul spirit can confuse pastors into believing that they are Jesus, or are mightier than their congregants and should be treated as such. Yet, their true role is to serve and introduce congregants to the Holy Spirit and create an atmosphere in which the Holy Spirit can thrive and be the deliverer and healer that He is.

It is the spirit that causes leaders to feel like they own a particular ministry, role, or title in the church. It is one of the main spirits that causes church folk to seemingly lose their minds in fighting, gossiping, and applying their personal beliefs instead of applying the Word of God in their positions in the church.

This is the spirit that causes church leaders to feel entitled to material things and believe that the congregation and leadership are there to serve them instead of the model Jesus created by serving the church. I am always a bit uncomfortable when I minister in churches around the country and they treat me like I am to be served, when I am there to serve. They save the best seats, food and have entire ministries dedicated to making me feel comfortable.

While I understand this, I have to be most careful not to allow the spirit of haughtiness to find an open door into my life. In other words, I cannot allow myself - for even one moment - to think that I am closer to God, or deserve extra special care because of a title or the pulpit I am standing behind.

This actually does the congregants a disservice because it sends an unspoken message that they are not as special to God and do not have access to the same teachings and the same Holy Spirit that the church leaders do. While I understand keeping the pastors and ministers freed up so they can lead their flock, you have to make sure that you are not leaving open doors for Satan to enter.

Haughtiness also shows up in your day-to-day life in ways you have been probably thinking were just a part of who you were. I realized that this was the case with me when I first went through the process of being cleaned.

This spirit keeps you blind to the fact that you even have a problem. You are not open to receiving any input or contribution. I could share story after story of "haughtiness gone wild," and I know you can too. However, I think you get the idea of how it shows up in your life. I have included many examples under each fruit, so you can notice this spirit working in your life.

The Fruit of the Spirit of Haughtiness

- ☐ Proud/Pride
- ☐ Scornful
- ☑ Mockery
- ☑ Judgment
- ☑ Gossip
- ☑ Ambition
- ☐ Love of position or social standing
- ☐ Loftiness
- ☐ Egotistical/ Egocentrism/Self-Centered
- ☐ Inter-church and inner-church competition
- ☐ Bragging/Boastfulness
- ☐ Stubborn/Obstinacy
- ☐ Arrogance

- ❏ Racism
- ❏ White supremacy
- ❏ Contention
- ❏ Self-righteousness
- ❏ Holier-than-thou
- ❏ Vanity
- ❏ Controlling/Domineering
- ❏ Self-assertion

How The Spirit of Haughtiness Enters

Haughtiness enters your life when you are not humble in a particular area. Believers were made so powerful in Jesus, it is easy to think that we are the source of our success and leave God out of the equation (Psalms 10:4). The moment we do this, it opens the door for this spirit to enter and wreak havoc.

Haughtiness must be recognized within someone and dealt with as soon as possible because it always leads to a downfall and disgrace. Scripture reminds us that:

> *Pride goes before destruction, a haughty spirit before*
> *a fall. – Proverbs 16:18*

This is why we are witnessing so many ministries being destroyed with open disgrace in the Body of Christ right now. God is calling His church back into order and the unclean must come out. Unfortunately, when we do not heed God's instructions on taking care of things privately, it then becomes a public issue to be dealt with.

Proud/Pride

Pride is the high or overbearing opinion of one's self-worth or importance and it a result of the spirit of haughtiness. I often hear people refer to a spirit of pride when they actually mean the spirit of haughtiness. Although pride will still respond when it is cast

2 forms of pride

out as a spirit, it does not remove the other fruit of this foul and offensive spirit.

There are two forms of pride you see in scripture. One of the forms of pride is associated with arrogance and loftiness. The other form of pride means majesty or ornament. They both lead down the same road and come from the same spirit of haughtiness. Confident people humbly know where their power and gifts come from and do not hesitate to give God the glory. Being prideful makes you think you are better than others.

Scornful

When you are harboring scorn, you refuse to do something because you perceive it as unworthy of who you believe yourself to be. You may even disown or shun that person or thing. Have you ever met someone who has disdain for his or her humble beginnings and disregards or disowns his or her family in scorn? Then you have met someone carrying this unclean fruit.

Mockery

As I get to each topic, God is dropping something in my mind to write about. The moment He dropped the instruction for this fruit, I said to myself, "Aw, do I have to, God?" I already know the answer to that.

In elementary school, I was deeply teased and ridiculed by my classmates. I used to dread recess because I knew it entailed being chased around the playground and being kicked in the butt as boys ran by yelling, "Big Butt!" or "Blubber Butt!" I remember being so used to being mocked by cruel names that one of my soccer teammate's older brothers used to call me, "Thunder Thighs," and I thought it was a compliment.

Ridiculing someone and making fun of them is mockery. It is rooted in the spirit of haughtiness and is cruel, which is not fun or of God. Mocking is not to be taken lightly because when it shows up in our children and is allowed to fester, they turn into cruel teenagers and adults who make fun of and taunt people around them. And yes, we even do it in the church.

Judgment

Judgment is a close relative of mockery. Judgment has become so common that I bet you are wondering if it is even possible to live without it. Yes, it is. It is so freeing to be rid of criticism and judgment, and a necessity for those seriously seeking to experience the Kingdom of God.

Unfortunately, one of the most judgmental places has become the church. When you judge others, it keeps you from completing the work Jesus expects of you. When you have time to judge someone else, you have taken your eyes off of God and put them on man. Honoring God is a full-time job and does not leave any time to even pay attention to what others are doing.

Gossip

Once someone begins judging someone else, the next expression of this spirit is that they begin gossiping and participating in unrestrained and ungodly talk about other people.

Just as I began to write on judgment, my phone rang and it was Veronica, one of my mentees, calling because she just left a meeting with her pastor. At the meeting, she shared her disappointment in his gossiping and slandering people in the church during the meetings she had with the church leadership as the head of the young adult ministry.

Remember, anytime the fruit of an unclean spirit is present, the stronghold spirit that produces that fruit is present within them, whether they are church leadership or not.

Ambition

When I first began this work in my life, I was shocked that ambition was even considered an unclean fruit. I honestly thought that it was a strong personality trait that I had and liked in myself and others.

In every list of characteristics that described who I was, I always listed "highly ambitious." Even in the first years of my ministry work, I was always pushing to make things happen. It was the model I grew up with from my father. I was taught that as long as I was capable of something, then I should push and make it happen. This is not Truth.

In the second and third year of my full-time ministry, I had a boyfriend, James, who actually pointed this out to me. He was very spiritual and had a gift for hearing from the Holy Spirit. He also happened to be the producer of the television show pilot I was working on. He just flowed and did not *make* anything happen and it used to drive me crazy. One day, I was pushing him to complete some work for a deadline I had created and he said to me, "Why can't you just let things happen? That's not God."

The haughty spirit I was carrying kicked up within me and I just said to myself, "He's a punk, he wouldn't understand." Oh, and did I mention that he actually had the same gifting of Jesus in that he could literally hear my thoughts. (Don't *ever* ask God for a man who can read your mind. It is not fun at all.) Anyway, I remember getting mad because he was implying that the way I was doing this work for God was not of God.

Once I was fully delivered from this spirit that had been able to run rampant in my life for as long as I could remember. I realized that he was right. Although I was doing the work of God, the pushing and over ambition was not of God, it was an unclean spirit. When you do something for God, it comes together with ease and flows with divine timing and order.

Love of position or social standing

I may be stepping on some toes with this form of ambition, but it is necessary if the church is going to be restored to what Jesus created it to be. We have become too attached to titles and positions within the church. We walk around acting like it is *our* choir, *our* praise and worship team, *our* auxiliary, and *our* ministry.

It is not yours; but, God's, and while you have been temporarily put in charge of it, it is only for a season while God grooms someone else for the position. It is of the devil when you believe it is yours. A church does not even belong to a pastor. It is God's.

It does not matter what title you have in the church. It does not matter what title you have at work. It is of the world to buy into the hierarchy of titles and positions and we get into trouble anytime you emulate the world in the Church or the Body of Christ. It gets you so stuck in tradition and ownership that you miss God.

I have witnessed people who were supposed to be church leadership, actually yelling at those whom God has sent to help a particular ministry, saying that, "This is my ministry, and this is how we do things." I steer clear of people too attached to title and position.

Loftiness

Have you ever walked into a room of women and they looked you up and down from toe to head and back again, without even greeting you? For years I thought this was jealousy, but it is loftiness, a fruit of the spirit of haughtiness. Haughtiness shows up in your eyes and you can see it in the other people's lofty looks. You may have called it, "someone looking down their nose at you," or "stuck up."

People who have a falsely elevated concept of who they are show their loftiness in their eyes. Another form of loftiness is when people wear sunglasses indoors and in places that are not appropriate or necessary for them. Success is a gift from God and does not give anyone the right to look down on anyone else.

Egotistical/ Ego-centrism/Self-Centered

I am trusting that you know whether or not you are self-centered and egotistical. If it is not natural for you to share and think of others before yourself, then you have a measure of this fruit flaring up in your life. It is time to let it go so you can be about the business of serving others.

Inter and inner-church competition

I have lost count of how many times I have been with church leadership that was visiting another church and commenting on something they saw that they would like in their own church.

We have choir competitions, preachers are trying to outdo one another and competition has become the norm in far too many churches. This breeds competition among the congregants and usually shows up in them trying to out dress or out serve each other. They are literally vying to get the attention of man and is of Satan.

Bragging/Boastfulness

I have understood for a long time that only insecure people brag. Secure people don't have to. They don't have anything to prove to anyone else and they just keep striving to walk with God and trying to fulfill their potential. Oxford dictionary actually defines boasting as, "talking about oneself with indulgent pride."

This includes bragging about your material possessions, the brand of your belongings, the university your child is attending or the vehicle you drive. The moment you brag, you are attempting to take God's glory and I wouldn't recommend it.

Stubborn/Obstinacy

As a child, I was told over and over that I was "hard-headed." I never wanted to listen to anything my parents or anyone else suggested. It kept me in trouble in school until I learned to channel it into student leadership where my stubbornness found a place to hide.

I thought that my stubborn ability to persist and hold on to building my ministry no matter what was a good thing. Then, I learned that persisting does not involve stubbornness and obstinacy, it is all about obedience. When you obey God, you will naturally flow in the things He asks of you, no matter what your circumstances look like. He will move everything out of the way for you. You don't have to stubbornly push or hold your ground. The Holy Spirit will lead you in knowing whether something is a test from God to endure or stubbornness operating within you.

Arrogance

A few of the synonyms for arrogance are assuming, conceited, egotistical, pompous, haughty and overbearing. One of the first things someone says when he or she encounters a person whose work is in the public-eye and are not arrogant is, "They are so down to earth." You actually can feel arrogance in someone and it is always a turn-off. Arrogance is a result of forgetting that all of the glory, honor and praise belongs to God.

Racism

Brace yourself for this one. As a matter of fact, sit down if you are not already sitting down. Yes, you read the list correctly. Racism is a spiritual issue.

When God was teaching me this, it absolutely blew me away! I was doing deliverances for two women, Debbie and Katie, over a period of two weeks. Up to that point, in the deliverance work, every unclean spirit I encountered fled no matter the race of the person being delivered. But for these two women, very minimal expulsion was occurring. I was absolutely baffled. After the customary two sessions, they were not experiencing deliverance.

I spent time in prayer repenting because I assumed that it was something in me and that I was impeding the process. I walked around quietly for two entire days just waiting for God to bring the revelation as to why this was happening in not one, but two women in the same week.

One morning I was eating my Rice Chex, when I heard, "The spirits are not moving because you are black." I almost choked on my food. "What!? Come again, God?"

He began to pour a revelation in me that rocked my world. He showed me glimpses into each of their families and their upbringings. He was showing me that there was extreme racism in both of their families and because the spirit of haughtiness was living in them, had seen me, and knew I was a black woman, it "felt" that it did not have to listen to me (as if it actually had rights, which it does not).

Both Debbie and Katie had turned away from this generational poison of their families. I asked God how I should proceed. He told me that I needed to share with them what He showed me. God also instructed me that I had to declare my position through Jesus and my authority to do this work as a black woman and that the stronghold spirit still had to obey the words I spoke.

I went back to both Debbie and Katie in our next sessions and explained the insight God had given me. They both shared how their families were racist and although they personally rejected it, they were brought up to believe that black people were inferior to white people.

Almost immediately after I declared my authority and that the spirits were still subject to the name of Jesus, the unclean spirits in both Debbie and Katie came out.

I would not have believed it unless I had witnessed it myself. It was at that moment that I realized that viewing one race as better than another is nothing more than fruit of the unclean spirit of haughtiness. That means that it can be cast down in others and cast out of you.

Since their deliverances, both Debbie and Katie reported that they have looked at other races with no judgment, scorn, or negative thoughts what-so-ever. To God be the glory!!!

White Supremacy

No need to expound on this fruit. Just apply everything I said in the description of racism.

Contention

The best word that captures the reality of contention is rivalry. Rivalry can only exist between people who are insecure and trying to define themselves through creating rivalries with others. I'm sure you can think of many examples in your work life of people who have created unspoken rivalries between one another.

I also know that if you thought about it, you can also think of rivalries occurring right now within your church. Can't we all just get along?

Self-righteousness

While there are many examples of self-righteousness in the world, it is not this self-righteousness that concerns me. I am concerned about the self-righteousness that believers carry. You become self-righteous when you compare your knowledge of God and scripture to others. You become the hypocritical judge and jury of people striving to live the precepts of God. Instead of assisting them in understanding the ways of God, you discredit and tune out what they are saying due to your self-righteousness.

Holier-than-thou

Have you ever interacted with a man or woman of God who cannot seem to get a word out without quoting scripture? While knowing scripture is wonderful, you feel something in your spirit that doesn't feel right about it. It actually felt like the person is trying to prove his or her holiness through his or her ability to quote scripture. It is not just the quoting of scripture, but the living of it that gets you closer to God. It is the Holy Spirit that leads and guides people to God. Anytime you attempt to impose your knowledge of the Word on someone, you have become Holier-than-thou and have crossed the line into unclean territory.

Vanity

In one of my adventures of watching reality TV, I ran across a show that is about getting clear about what real beauty is. The contestants on this reality TV show thought they were selected solely for their physical beauty when indeed they were being judged based on their inner beauty.

I sat in disbelief as the contestants had their one-on-one with the camera and described how they were the most gorgeous person in the world. Each and every one of them sincerely believed that their appearance was superior to everyone else's. They were shocked to find out that the cameras were rolling as they put others down, gossiped and spewed conceit behind everyone else's back. Their vanity stopped them from seeing the best in people and focusing on the higher things of God.

Controlling/Domineering

When people attempt to manage your life without your permission, they are responding to the presence of the spirit of haughtiness within them. You cannot be controlling and domineering without being judgmental and feeling that your way is better than anyone else's. Another name that is often used to describe controlling and domineering people is "bossy." This, too, is not of God.

Self-assertion

In every workshop I have ever conducted since I was in my late teens, there has always been a person who loves to suck up all of the energy, time, and attention with incessant questions. They hide behind thinking that they are asserting themselves in a good way, but it is evident to everyone in the room that they have issues.

You can lovingly have boundaries that enable you to be respected and honored without aggressively or forcefully imposing yourself on others. People who are truly confident and know who they are in Christ do not have to be loud and draw attention to him or herself. When you are authentically confident and trust in Jesus, you don't have to say a word.

That does it for the spirit of haughtiness. Let's move on to a very common stronghold in the lives of believers, lying spirit.

LYING SPIRIT

When I began my professional coach training over eight years ago, they taught us that there was a term for negative self-talk called "gremlins." We were taught that when someone speaks something other than what they truly desire, it is their "gremlin" talking and not their truth.

They were on to something. In Truth, while it isn't really a gremlin, it is an unclean spirit trying to stop you from doing what God called you to do and being who He created you to be.

Lying spirit tells you that you aren't good enough, you can't do it, you don't have enough money, it will never work and if you try, you will fail. It goes on and on until it literally talks you out of even trying. There are many faces of lying spirit.

When I encounter lying spirit during deliverance, the Holy Spirit allows me to hear what it is saying. It always influences the other unclean spirits and tries to convince them that they do not have to come out. In order to get lying spirit out, you have to understand how it is showing up in your life.

The Fruit of the Lying Spirit

- ☐ Lies
- ☐ Exaggerating/Stretching the truth
- ☐ Little "white" lies
- ☐ Strong delusion
- ☐ Manipulation
- ☐ Deceit
- ☐ Flattery
- ☐ Vain Babbling/Excessive talking
- ☑ Profanity
- ☐ Hypocrisy
- ☐ Religious Spirit/Condemning spirit

- ❏ Frenzied emotional actions
- ❏ Old Wives' tales/fables
- ❏ Superstitions
- ❏ Vain Imagination/Notions (rejects the Truth of God)

How Lying Spirit Enters

Lying spirit finds a home in your temple when you are not feeling safe or supported. It enters into someone usually with feelings of low self-esteem. This low self-esteem opens the door for lying spirit to come in. Then, it begins lying and the games begin.

Lies

While I think you already know what a lie is, I just want to make sure it is thoroughly defined. A lie is an intentionally false or deceptive statement. When lying is allowed to permeate someone's temple, the liar actually begins to convince him or herself that the lie is truth.

When I used to watch criminal investigation shows (before I realized that they were opening the door to unclean spirits), I used to always be amazed at how almost every person accused of the crime lies - even if he or she committed it. It takes diligent research and detective work to actually produce evidence before someone will actually get caught in his or her lie and tell the truth.

Exaggerating/Stretching the Truth

We did a personality assessment at my former church. One of the personality profiles, called Influencer, listed exaggeration as a character trait. We laughingly call it "stretching the truth" but indeed it is not of God. Before I learned the stronghold spirits and their fruits, I did not understand that this is actually an unclean spirit and not part of someone's "colorful" personality.

Little "white" lies

There is no need to go into much detail on this one, it is worth noting that there is no such thing as a small lie or what we call "little white" lies. When the Holy Spirit lives in you and the unclean spirits are out, you will not be able to lie.

Strong Delusion

This fruit refers to someone who enjoys leading people astray and leaving a false impression of themselves or a situation. If gone undetected, delusion can turn into psychological challenges. Either way, it is a spiritual issue.

Allow the Holy Spirit to guide you in discerning if someone is carrying delusion. Satan is the master of delusion and once this fruit is growing in your life, it is difficult to reel it back in. It is absolutely necessary to cast it out so you can take off the masks and live right.

Manipulation

A manipulator is someone who twists situations to his or her own advantage. I prefer that people come right out and let me know what they want, rather than trying to insinuate and imply what it is that they want. As a matter of fact, I really don't know of any examples to share here because the people in my life are rather straightforward. I'm sure you can think of some people who have the challenge of being manipulative and twisting things around to get what they want. I'll leave this one up to you.

Deceit

A former acquaintance of mine was a master of deception and he targeted his church as his prey. He masqueraded as a concerned financial advisor and real estate agent and manipulated more than fifty families to sign over their homes to his company.

While I don't know all of the details, I do know that many people were financially ruined by his deceit.

The thing about deceit is that those who do the deceiving are very charming, just as Satan himself was before he was cast out of Heaven. With the Holy Spirit, these people can be fully detected before you get involved with them.

> *Your heart became proud on account of your beauty,*
> *and you corrupted your wisdom because of your*
> *splendor. – Ezekial 28:17*

Flattery

Flattery is not to be confused with giving sincere compliments. Someone moving in flattery tells people something to manipulate them for his or her selfish purpose, gain, or advantage. It is exaggerated or insincere acclaim. A common name we call someone who is a flatterer is a "brown-noser." Now that's something you can relate to, right?

Vain Babbling/Excessive talking

When you have a conversation with someone who excessively uses the word "I," it is a turn-off. This behavior shields people from showing his or her real self. I have witnessed God closing the lips of someone with vain babbling based on my speaking to it in the name of Jesus. Next time you are with someone who is manifesting this fruit, just quietly cast down lying spirit and you'll be just fine.

Profanity

Cursing is not of God. Fussing people is not of God. The Word clearly states that blessings and curses should not come from the same mouth (James 3:10). Profanity is the fruit of a lying spirit. Once your heart and spirit are cleansed, you will not be able to be in the presence of cursing. The cursing upsets your spirit and you become highly sensitive to anything unclean.

> *What goes into a man's mouth does not make him 'unclean,' but what comes out of his mouth, that is what makes him 'unclean.' – Matthew 15:11*

I was having a conversation with Katrina, a student of my ministry, who attended my most recent retreat She began sharing how she had no tolerance for cursing in her presence, yet her co-workers cursed on a regular basis. I walked her through the process of casting down the lying spirit in her co-workers and told her that once she commanded the unclean spirits in the name of Jesus, they will not be able to curse in her presence. She applied the teaching and ceased having issues with her coworkers.

[handwritten margin note: casting down]

Hypocrisy

It doesn't take long to see the hypocrisy that is running rampant, not only in the world but in the church. Just this evening as I was watching the news, they posted the picture of a pastor who was accused of raping a sixteen year old member of his congregation. The stories could go on and on. And those are only the stories that make the news.

These are the most heart-breaking stories because we deeply want to believe in the holiness of our church leaders. No matter what title someone has, or the amount of power and influence he or she has, it is not of God to teach and do one thing publicly and do the opposite of that teaching privately. Jesus is clearing out hypocrisy from His church.

In one of Apostle Elijah Forte's teachings on church leadership, he talks about what happens when there is hypocrisy in marriages within the church. He shares:

> *When you are married and you come to church and you are all "churchy" and your spouse is sitting right*

there with you and they know how you act at home,
that man or that woman who is your spouse is the
one who is going to stand at the judgment seat
against you because "the real you" is at home.

There is a high price to pay for being a hypocrite.

Religious spirit/Condemning spirit

Another word for someone manifesting this aspect of lying spirit is a person who pretends that they are living free from sin. It reminds me of when Jesus asked the person who is free from sin to cast the first stone at the adulterous woman and no could (John 8:7). It is the act of a condemning or an overly religious spirit. The Holy Spirit is loving, gentle, and kind, not condemning.

Frenzied emotional actions

When I saw that Mary Garrison, the author of *How To Try A Spirit*, listed this manifestation as a form of lying spirit, I was not clear about what she meant, until I asked the Holy Spirit to help me understand.

He showed me an image of people running around the church, supposedly being moved by the Holy Spirit. The hollering, yelling, and seemingly uncontrollable actions of people who are said to be feeling "the spirit" are not actually feeling the Holy Spirit at all, but lying spirit. Remember, the Holy Spirit comes like a dove and leads you to still waters. He is not loud and boisterous in the way He moves.

I have come to learn that when people put on this "holy" act, it is actually their unclean spirits fighting against the Holy Spirit and not the Holy Spirit itself. Hmmm...

Old Wives Tales/Fables

As I was sharing this fruit at a recent retreat at which I was teaching, I shared the old wives tales and fables that they were raised with and it was truly laughable. They started naming tales ranging from not stepping on a crack to avoid breaking your mother's back to having to throw salt over your shoulder and turn around in a three hundred sixty degree circle when you forget something and have to run back in the house to get it. They are all lies. Jesus is the only way to the full enlightenment of God. There is no one, no action, or no object that can get you closer to Jesus.

Superstitions

The same goes for superstitions that have been passed down from generation to generation. Some of the most familiar superstitions are:

- Friday, the thirteenth, is an unlucky day.
- A rabbit's foot brings good luck.
- Wearing the same piece of clothes under your sports uniform brings good luck.
- To find a four-leaf clover is to find good luck.
- If you walk under a ladder, you will have bad luck.
- If a black cat crosses your path you will have bad luck.
- To break a mirror will bring you seven years of bad luck.
- To open an umbrella in the house is to bring bad luck.
- You can break a bad luck spell by turning seven times in a clockwise circle.
- Garlic protects from evil spirits.
- Wearing your birthstone will bring you good luck.
- If you blow out all of the candles on your birthday cake with the first breath you will get whatever you wish for.

No matter how long they have been passed on through generations, each of these superstitions is a lie. The name of Jesus is the name above all names (Phil 2:9) and none of these superstitions control the power of God. Your power lies in the name of Jesus, not in any superstitious beliefs.

Vain Imagination/Notions (rejects the Truth of God)

Mary Garrison said it best when I first saw her description of this manifestation in her book *How to Try A Spirit*. I would like to share her words:

> Many of us are, or have been, guilty of this without realizing it. For example: we imagine what the end time will be like; and we form some sort of notion of opinion without actually studying all the Word reveals about it. We accept that sort of notion, or vain imagination, as the truth. Then when we hear someone state a truth concerning it, it is so foreign to us that we reject it as being far-out. Sometimes we actually state our vain notice as a truth.

I also see this dimension of lying spirit when believers covet the callings and vision of others. This causes you to create imaginings of what your life could be like if you did what they do. You may see someone with a television ministry and begin to imagine the fame it may bring you and move on it without it being an instruction from the Lord.

God's vision for your life chooses you. You don't choose it. God will give you glimpses of what is to come to keep you on the right path and then give you the steps to move forward in faith. You then use your imagination to stretch your mind around the images God provides for you, not fictitious ones that you made up.

All right, I think you are clear about lying spirit. Let's move on.

PERVERSE SPIRIT

Perverse spirit is one of the "meanest" of the unclean spirits. I have gotten a chance to deliver many people from perverse spirit and it has come out screeching every time. In addition to being one of the meanest unclean spirits, it can cause the most damage to a person's mind, body, soul, and spirit.

It leaves you feeling like you are dirty and incapable of being fully loved. It keeps you profoundly oppressed. No matter how hard you try to operate on top of it, you always feel stuck, unlovable, and feeling inadequate in every area of your life.

The good news is that you are about to get free from perverse spirit. It has to be cast out and expelled and it may go kicking and screaming – literally.

In a deliverance session I was doing with Charlene, the perverse spirit within her was literally feeding on the unforgiveness she was holding for her ex-husband, who brutally beat her every day they were together. In addition to beating her every day, his perverse spirit forced her to participate in perverted sexual acts. With her being incestuously molested as a child and having the man who was supposed to love and protect her treating her so violently, she had become a master at covering up her abuse. Her closest friends did not even know she was being beaten on a daily basis.

As she was releasing the deep unforgiveness she had for her ex-husband the perverse spirit attached to the unforgiveness came out simultaneously. We were doing this work over the phone and I remember thinking that the noises that were coming out of her were unlike anything I had ever heard. What began as crying (spirit of heaviness was manifesting), quickly turned into coughing.

The coughs continued until she was heaving. Within minutes, her heaving turned into an inhuman screeching noise that went longer than any person could have mustered. I was listening intently and wondering how she was able to catch her breath in the midst of the screeches coming up out of her. I commanded the perverse spirit to stop manifesting so she could catch her breath and I could check in with her and see how she was doing.

She was shocked, but fine, and we continued the session until the spirit had fully been expelled. The Holy Spirit always shows me in the spirit what is happening with the unclean spirits. I knew that any stronghold spirits that had attached themselves to perverse spirit were also being expelled.

That night, Charlene had the best night of sleep she had ever had. We hadn't even gotten to the second session in which Jesus expels the remaining unclean spirits from her. The second session was a similar release and she is now completely free from all unclean spirits and is diligently working on her life's vision. Before our work, she was not able to focus and could not see what God called her to do clearly.

She attended the last meeting of Touch and AGree, the Professional Christian Women's Network meeting I co-founded, and she had a glow. She was literally radiating the glory of God! When we hugged and I asked her how she was doing, she was giggling and said, "Vision full-steam ahead, drama gone!" To God be the glory!!!

The Fruit of Perverse Spirit

- ❏ Wounded spirit
- ❏ Severe self-esteem issues
- ❏ Snare
- ❏ Perverse words/Fool

- ❏ Extreme lust
- ❏ Perverting the gospel
- ❏ Rebellion
- ❏ Sexual violence
- ❏ Extreme pornography addiction and role playing
- ☑ Masturbation
- ❏ False teaching
- ❏ Rape
- ❏ Incest
- ❏ Molestation
- ❏ Homosexuality
- ❏ Incubus and Succubus

How Perverse Spirit Enters

Perverse spirit enters when you have been sexually violated. It also enters into your life through fornication, or repeated exposure to pornographic images. It can be through molestation, rape or the most diabolical of all – incest. It is the most oppressive in children who have been incestuously molested. If you experienced molestation by a family member, it is more damaging because the violation came from someone who was supposed to love and protect you.

It can also enter in your teen or adult years through fornication and repeated exposure to sex or pornography. All too often, it runs down family lines and is therefore a generational curse. No matter how old you are, when perverse spirit has found an open door into your life, it is very difficult to live with.

If perverse spirit is allowed to go undetected until well into your adult life, it most often shows up in extremely poor choices in romantic relationships. Those who are carrying perverse spirit tend to gravitate toward emotionally and physically abusive relationships.

In a deliverance session I was doing for Delores, she shared that in her preschool years, her daycare provider would sit her and the other kids in front of pornographic movies for hours everyday. As a result, the children began repeating what they saw on the movies with one another. The daycare provider convinced the children that they liked it, and if they ever told their parents, she would tell them that they liked it and they would be in trouble. They never told.

You can't even imagine the doors that this opened in Delores' life. It was amazing to watch God free her from the wrath of the perverse spirit she encountered as a young girl.

Perverse spirit perpetuates itself through generation after generation. Everyone who I have worked with who had this spirit in their temples suffered at the hands of someone else who had also encountered an expression of perversity.

Wounded Spirit

There is something about experiencing sexual violation that wounds the survivor to the core of their very being. The damage that occurs after this spirit has ravaged a life is great. When you have a wounded spirit, there is nothing that anyone else can tell you or you can get from the world that convinces you that you are worthy and can move forward unscathed.

I just praise the name of Jesus that He has provided a way for you to be fully released from this trauma that can leave its scar on every area of your life.

Severe self-esteem issues

As a result of the deep wounds that sexual violation causes, severe self-esteem issues are created in the life of the survivor. This is not just low self-esteem, these are severe self-esteem issues that leave a gaping hole in a person's soul and spirit.

No matter what the world sees when it looks at someone who has lived through perverse spirit's violation, the person feels dirty, unworthy, and sees him or herself as unattractive. Survivors of perversion can think that it was something that they did to deserve or attract the sexual violation. Either way it shows up in your life, it leaves destruction in its wake.

Snare

When I think of a snare, I think of a trap that is set in a hidden place that pulls a person into its grasp. That is exactly what someone does when they are carrying perverse spirit. He or she can set out to deliberately lure you into their perversion. He or she can weave a sticky web that can pull you into error, if you are not prayed up and listening to the leading of the Holy Spirit.

Perverse words/Fool

When I first moved to North Carolina, I was blown away to meet so many "men of God," who used foul and perverted language to try to get me to get physical with them. They would quote scripture and share the church they attended and then proceed to act just like the men I used to meet in the world.

When my flesh died to this activity, I ceased responding and they were obviously at a loss as to how to react to my lack of interest. Without me even saying a word, they just vaporized from my life because the darkness they brought had no place in my life.

I have learned to just let these perverse men reveal who they are through their words and actions. Their improper actions truly make them a fool (a person who acts unwisely) and God will deal with them accordingly.

Extreme lust

When you cannot even walk by someone of the opposite sex without looking them up and down and resting your gaze upon their chest and booty, you know you have an extreme lust problem. In the days when I used to "club" every weekend, this was rampant. It was normal for you to walk by a man and he would stop in his tracks, watch the sway of your hips and breasts as you walked by (now you know I was swaying even more on purpose back in those days, right?) and uncontrollably holler, "Damn!"

It is not a normal reaction to behave like this. We often chalk it up to someone just being "fine," but the true issue is that you cannot see beyond someone's physical appearance when you are overcome with extreme lust. This is the spirit that is fed during every one-night stand around the world.

Perverting the gospel

Immediately, a particular memory strikes me for this description. I was up late one Saturday night and happened to turn to a show called *Cheaters*. It is a show that confronts the significant others of those who suspect they are being cheated on. In this particular clip of this episode the cameras found the significant other at a Bible study.

Their Bible study was peculiar. They were involved in having sex as they read the gospel. But the part that shocked me was that the leader of this sect of so-called Christians was saying to the camera, "What? God created sex and pleasure for us to enjoy. We are not doing anything but worshipping God."

[Silence]. I don't have anything else to say about this one.

Rebellion

When you think of rebellion, it may bring to mind an image of a member of a biker gang who has openly rebelled against society and follows a path of nomads living in seedy motel rooms across the country. This is only one extreme example of how rebellion can show up.

Rebellion can also rear up its ugly head in everything from the pastor's children, to the business owner who dropped out of college and created an empire in his or her own way.

In believers, it shows up when you go against the Word or pick and choose the aspects of the Word that work for you and discard the rest. In whatever form it comes, rebellion occurs when you go against the authority of God, or the governing body of whatever establishment that impacts your life. God requires you to separate from the world and draw closer to Him. Rebellion separates you from God.

Sexual violence

This spirit of perversion often shows up violently and gains pleasure from hurting people. We can even give this expression of perversion cute names like a "freak."

I was sitting with a powerful woman of God who used to be married to an anointed man of God. She shared with me that the more anointed the man is, the more freaky he is in the bed. She said that she really struggled with this when she was married as a woman of God. While she did not go into detail, I knew she was referring to potentially violent sexual acts. Wherever there is sexual violence, there is evidence of the presence of perverse spirit.

Extreme pornography addiction and role playing

Anytime you give into the urgings of your flesh, it takes you away from the Spirit of God. Romans reminds you:

> *For they that are after the flesh do mind the things of the flesh; but they that are after the Spirit the things of the Spirit. – Romans 8:5*

One of Satan's most common tricks against you is to appeal to the flesh's nature to give into sinful pleasure. I have been out of high school for a long time and I still remember the first time that I attended a house party where the guys were watching "XXX-rated" movies as they sat and ate chips and dip like it was nothing.

This opened my eyes to this being perceived as normal among many men. I remember having male friends in college that had prized collections of pornographic videos (this was pre-DVD) that they exchanged with one another like any other video. Pornography is designed to pull you in and you're your flesh desire and repeat what is on the screen.

I work with many women who share that their husbands have an addiction to pornography. I also work with men who have come to a place in their walk with God to admit that they have an addiction to porn and are ready to get it out of their lives for good. I always tell them that the first thing they have to do is throw away all of their sexual paraphernalia and begin to starve out their perverse spirit. When you are addicted, that is not easy to do. Once you stop feeding the spirit, it must be cast out in order for you to be truly free.

Masturbation

Masturbation has infiltrated the lives of believers so much that I have even heard single believers share that their church leadership actually taught them that masturbation is okay because it keeps them from sinning sexually. This is not true.

Masturbation actually opens the door for perverse spirit to come in and increase your sexual appetite until you then begin to use sexual toys. Then, eventually, you will no longer be able to fight it before you will seek out other believers carrying this spirit and begin to fornicate together.

Long before I was delivered from the spirit of lust, I remember actually going with a girlfriend to a sex store to shop for sex toys. This wasn't just any small sex store. It was the only business located in a three-story building. I have only been in a few of these stores in my past, but I remember being shocked that this store had an entire wall of different types of vibrators. The customer service woman was giving us an overview of the features of each model, as if we were shopping for a new car and it was perfectly normal.

I want to add here that it is not of God for adolescent boys or men to masturbate either. It is still a manifestation of perverse spirit and must be cast out before their sexual appetite becomes unquenchable.

You can truly be free of the lust that leads to masturbation so it never crosses your mind. I just praise God for Him giving us the power, authority, and dominion to cast this wretched spirit from our lives.

False teaching

There is also a form of perverting the gospel when false teachers and prophets twist and manipulate the Word of God. I think of the many cults and religious movements that have preyed on followers and perverted the Word of God, in the name of racism, violence, suicide, control, and sexual sin.

The Word tells you how to recognize a false teacher.

> *But there were also false prophets among the people, just as there will be false teachers among you. They will secretly introduce destructive heresies, even denying the sovereign Lord who bought them— bringing swift destruction on themselves.*
>
> *Many will follow their shameful ways and will bring the way of truth into disrepute. In their greed these teachers will exploit you with stories they have made up. Their condemnation has long been hanging over them, and their destruction has not been sleeping. – 2 Peter 2:1-3*

Rape

I don't think it takes much to explain rape. It is the act of forcing a person to have sexual intercourse or performing sexual acts against his or her will. Because of the presence of perverse spirit in the rapist, it is passed to the person being raped. When a rapist sexually violates a child before they are even aware of what sex is, it is incest and molestation.

Incest and molestation

Incest is one of the most hideous manifestations of any unclean spirit. It is rape and/or sexual violation that is perpetrated on another family member. The wake of this unclean act is profoundly damaging because someone in your own family that you should be able to trust does the ultimate act of filth against you.

There is something even deeper about incest that leaves scars. The understanding of this aspect of incest came from my childhood best friend, Charlotte. I shared her story earlier. She was repeatedly raped and molested by her older step brother during a period of time that he lived with her family. She tried to share it with her mother and father and they did not believe her, nor did they limit his access to her.

Whenever the family was leaving to run errands, he would suggest that he and Charlotte stay at the house until they return. She always knew what would happen next and felt shamed, trapped, and perpetually dirty.

We often talked about this during the endless summer days we spent bike riding and exercising. Then one day as she was progressing in her healing process, she shared with me the key to her healing.

One day, I was at her house and we were playing a game of *Monopoly*. Somewhere in-between Park Place and Baltic Avenue, she casually said, "Ericka, do you know the worst part about what happened to me? It's that my body reacted." She went on to explain the deep shame and confusion she experienced because, while she knew what was happening was wrong, her flesh reacted.

That always stuck with me. Even until last January when I was speaking at a women's retreat. God released the spirit of healing and women began to come forward one-by-one to share their horrendous experiences of being raped and sexually violated. There was one very strong and well-known woman who came forth to share and admitted that every summer when she traveled down south to be with her grandparents, her uncle repeatedly raped her. She had not said a word about it for more than forty years.

Later, we both happened to be getting drinks at the lunch-time drink station. I commented that she looked younger and her energy felt lighter. She said half to me and half to herself, "I wonder why I held on to that and did not tell anyone for so many years."

I shared what my friend Charlotte shared with me over that *Monopoly* game and she said, "That's it! I didn't tell anyone because I felt so ashamed that my body reacted." Once she shared it, she felt so free!

Homosexuality

The Word does share how God began to allow homosexuality and what happens when it is allowed to take root in someone's life. Like every other unclean spirit, it is not of God and while we try to justify homosexual behavior as the norm now, I am clear that when people say, "I was born this way," that they are unknowingly referring to a generational perverse spirit in their family line. Homosexuality is not a spirit, it is the fruit of perverse spirit and must be called out correctly in order to leave. Here is what the Word has to say about it:

Therefore God gave them over in the sinful desires of their hearts to sexual impurity for the degrading of their bodies with one another. They exchanged the truth of God for a lie, and worshiped and served created things rather than the Creator—who is forever praised. Amen.

Because of this, God gave them over to shameful lusts. Even their women exchanged natural relations for unnatural ones. In the same way the men also abandoned natural relations with women and were inflamed with lust for one another. Men committed indecent acts with other men, and received in themselves the due penalty for their perversion.

Furthermore, since they did not think it worthwhile to retain the knowledge of God, he gave them over to a depraved mind, to do what ought not to be done. They have become filled with every kind of wickedness, evil, greed and depravity. – Romans 1:24-28

Incubus and succubus

Incubus is an unclean spirit that accesses women's dreams. A succubus is a demon who takes the form of a highly attractive woman to seduce men in their dreams to have sexual intercourse. Their male counterpart is the incubus.

I had never heard of either one of these unclean spirits until one evening at Bible Study. My former pastor mentioned them in a study he was doing on the sins of the father. He talked about how they can come to you in a dream in the form of male or female genitals. I never knew such a thing existed. Then, I experienced it.

I woke up one morning after I was delivered and just sat on the edge of my bed in amazement. I had just had a dream that a gigantic penis was laying on the pillow next to me. As soon as I woke up I knew exactly what was going on. I was baffled because this should not have been the case once the spirit of lust and perverse spirit was cast out of my temple.

Then it hit me, I cast them out of my body, spirit, soul and mind, but I did not cast them out of my dreams. Prior to this, I hadn't had sexual dreams in years. As I sat on the edge of my bed, I began to speak to the unclean perverse spirit and commanded it to come out of my dreams, as well as the part of my body that dreamed and never return again. Immediately, I started the deep yawning that I have come to call a 'deliverance yawn.' After three huge yawns, I knew that incubus was gone from my life forever.

Okay, now that we have perverse spirit out of the way, let us move on to spirit of divination.

SPIRIT OF DIVINATION

It is quite easy to determine the presence of the spirit of divination. This spirit is working when you look to anything for insight from God, other than Jesus. It is occurring when we give objects the power, when the true power lies only in the name of Jesus and the Holy Spirit.

It is also present when you look to people to give you the insight that you should be seeking from the Holy Spirit. As much as I do not want to admit it, in my years of running from Jesus, I participated in many forms of divination. All of these are considered abominations to the Lord:

> *There shall not be found among you any one that maketh his son or his daughter to pass through the fire, or that useth divination, or an observer of times, or an enchanter, or a witch.*
>
> *Or a charmer, or a consulter with familiar spirits, or a wizard, or a necromancer.*
>
> *For all that do these things are an abomination unto the LORD: and because of these abominations the LORD thy God doth drive them out from before thee.*
> *– Deut 18: 10 – 12 KJ.*

I remember receiving a deck of Lakota Sweat Lodge cards as a going away present when I moved back home from Washington, DC to Seattle. I would sit for hours doing different card spreads, seeking insight and revelation from the cards. I had no idea that I was opening up all kinds of doors through which Satan could gain footholds in my life. It wasn't long after that that I began to experience a depression that lasted for more than two years.

I don't even have time to mention the various "new age" books I had in my possession at that time in my life. I considered my books as one of my most prized possessions and moved them from coast-to-coast with me. Then one day I heard the Holy Spirit ask me, "Why are you running from me?" I had to ask myself why I was so willing to be open to what these books were saying about God but I was rebelling (spirit of haughtiness) against the Word of Jesus.

I then came back to my senses and got back into the Word and the deeper things of Jesus. I threw away all books that were not of Jesus. In all of my delving into "spiritual" things, it led me right back to Jesus as the only way. Remember, people can claim anything in the name of God, but they can only claim the truth in the name of Jesus. Trust me on this one, I've tried.

> *Jesus answered, "I am the way and the truth and the life. No one comes to the Father except through me. –*
> *John 14:6*

After I fully surrendered, I finally deeply and profoundly understood the scripture that declares that Jesus is the only true way to God. All "spiritual" teachings claim to be about God, but it is not the Truth if it is not of Jesus.

All "spiritual" teachings claim to be about God but it is not the Truth if it is not of Jesus.

The Fruit of the Spirit of Divination
- ❏ Diviner
- ❏ Psychics
- ❏ Enchanter/Magician
- ❏ Witch or wizard
- ❏ Hypnotist
- ❏ Familiar spirits

- ❏ Mediums
- ☑ Clairvoyant
- ❏ Necromancer/Ancestor worshiper
- ☑ Conjurer
- ❏ Palm Readers
- ❏ Star gazer/Worshiper
- ❏ Astrologers
- ❏ Fortune Tellers/Crystal Balls
- ❏ Good luck charms, pendulums, etc.
- ❏ Angel Worshiper

How the Spirit of Divination Enters

The spirit of divination looks for symbols and objects that open the way to your vulnerability. It may enter through a mask or trinket you brought back from your travels without understanding what was attached to that mask. It waits for you to turn to symbols and objects to hear from God and then gains a foothold into your life.

We even have to be careful with the objects we use in the church that symbolize the presence of God. The first one that comes to mind is our use of olive oil. While olive oil represents the Holy Spirit, it has no power of its own. It is the application in the midst of the name of Jesus that gives it symbolized power. Anytime you put a symbol or object above the power of Jesus, you open the door for this deceitful and wicked spirit to grow roots in your life.

Diviner

A diviner is someone who has a gift of seeing into the spiritual realm and uses it for Satan or the world. While it is a gift, the question is, "What is the gift being used for?" If someone is not saved and using their gift to impact the world and not the Kingdom of God, then it is of Satan. This can be a hard concept to get because there are so many "new age" and other philosophies that appear to be doing good, but they are being used to build the world and not God's Kingdom.

It is only a gift of God when someone is using it to build God's Kingdom through Jesus Christ. Anything else is something you definitely want to stay away from.

It is only a gift of God when someone is using it to build God's Kingdom through Jesus Christ. Anything else is something you definitely want to stay away from.

Psychics

The world looks to psychics to share possibilities of their future because it does not have access to the Holy Spirit. I remember being curious back in the eighties and calling an 1-800 number psychic hotlines. The women told me that she saw me getting a job in a bar. As hard as I tried not to laugh on the line, I broke out in a fit of laughter because she was so far off. If she only knew that I do not do alcohol and would never even consider working in that environment – ever.

I think my Oxford dictionary says it best when it refers to a psychic as "A person considered to have occult powers, such as telepathy, clairvoyance, or mind reading. "For every true gift from God, Satan has an imposter. A psychic is Satan's imposter for a believer who has the gift of discernment and prophecy.

For every true gift from God, Satan has an imposter.

Something as common as reading your horoscope can provide a crack in the door just long enough for an unclean spirit to sneak in.

Enchanter/Magician

The Word also mentions enchanters or magicians as those wicked kings and pharaohs whose hearts had hardened from the things of God (Exodus 7:22) turned to for advice and insight. Time and time again in the Word, their skills were not able to rival the signs and wonders of God. Enchanters and magicians went to great lengths to attempt to impersonate the signs and wonders of God.

> *The king talked with them, and he found none equal to Daniel, Hananiah, Mishael and Azariah; so they entered the king's service. In every matter of wisdom and understanding about which the king questioned them, he found them ten times better than all the magicians and enchanters in his whole kingdom. – Daniel 1:19*

They are still going strong these days. They are at fairs, carnivals, festivals, and theme parties and just about anywhere else you can think of.

Witch or wizard

Thanks to the world of reality TV, I have gotten a glimpse into the fact that there are people right now who believe they are witches and the male counterpart, wizards, in Pagan (includes Wiccan) religions. A witch is defined by Oxford as a woman supposed to have dealings with the devil or evil spirits. A pagan is defined as a nonreligious person; pantheist (worship that admits or tolerates all gods); heathen.

To this day there are meet-up groups for witches around the world. The Word clearly states that witchcraft is a sin (1 Samuel 15:23). It is listed as a work of flesh that will not inherit the Kingdom of God (Galatians 5:20-21).

Hypnotist

Even if it is for entertainment purposes only, dealing with a hypnotist is a form of Satanic expression. Hypnotists impose a sleep-like state, in which their subject acts only on external suggestion. Used in the area of psychotherapy, it may be used to access a patient's subconscious thoughts, usually related to a personal trauma they have survived.

Again, this is something that the Holy Spirit will do for you. As I have learned to walk in my gifts from God, I can actually look at someone and the Holy Spirit will share the trauma that he or she experienced. This experience is not unique to me, it is true for anyone I have met who walks fully in the gift of deliverance. This is a gift that all believers should be walking in.

This gift is indispensible when I coach because God literally shows me the past of those He sends to me to help navigate their way to His vision for their lives. I am fully aware that unclean spirits attach to one another and there is never just one in operation. It is The Holy Spirit that will show you everything you need to know without ever having to work with hypnotism.

Familiar spirits

Familiar spirit is a stronghold spirit but because it is such a close relative to spirit of divination, I have combined it with this section other than list it as its own stronghold spirit. I will turn to

Mary Garrison's words from *How to Try a Spirit* to distinguish the description of a familiar spirit.

> Those who possess a familiar spirit call it a personal spirit guide, who is friendly and on intimate terms with the person possessing him. He is a servant to be summoned at will. He is often passed on in a family, down through generations.

Medium – consults with familiar spirits

Mediums have become so popular that they frequently make appearances on talk shows and I have seen some of them with their own TV shows. There is even a TV show on the NBC network called *Medium*. A medium is a person who is a means for messages to be communicated with familiar spirits. Their gifts are used for the world and the people in it, it is not of Jesus.

Clairvoyant

The world calls clairvoyance the supposed ability to perceive things or events in the future and beyond normal sensory contact. As with every manifestation of the spirit of divination, clairvoyance is Satan's counterfeit version of discernment and prophecy.

Necromancer/Ancestor worship

CBS network has a show centered around necromancy, *Ghost Whisperer*. Mediums are also forms of necromancers (Deut 18:11), people who consult the dead for insight and understanding. When you look around at the fact that it is common in cultures to have statues and monuments of dead people, you can see just how pervasive this spirit is.

When I used to attend African dance classes and events, I had no idea that I was opening the door to the spirit of divination. Every event used to begin with libation where we called out the names of our ancestors. We called on them to give us strength and wisdom because it is them on whose shoulders we stand. Giving honor to past loved ones and calling on their spirit to show up are two different things.

While this sounds harmless, I was opening the door that could allow Satan to drive a wedge between me and the only name that he bows to – Jesus.

Conjurer

The best image of a conjurer that comes to mind is associated with voodoo. I just had an image of Diahann Carroll's character, Elzora, in *Eve's Bayou* as she used a voodoo doll to cast a death spell on Samuel Jackson's character, Louis Batiste. Conjurers call upon evil spirits to appear.

Palm Readers

This is another form of consulting things in the natural realm to gain insight, understanding or knowledge of the future. Palmistry can trace its roots back to Indian (Hindu) Astrology (known in Sanskrit as Jyotish) and gypsy fortune tellers. It is an occult practice of darkness that like all other manifestations of this spirit opens the door to unclean spirits moving into your temple.

Star gazer/worshiper

While God created the stars of the universe, it is important to always go directly to the Creator by way of the Holy Spirit to explore the things of Heaven. The Word reminds us:

> And when you look up to the sky and see the sun, the moon and the stars—all the heavenly array—do not be enticed into bowing down to them and worshiping things the LORD your God has apportioned to all the nations under heaven. – Deut 4:19

Astrologers

While there were soothsayers and astrologers in the Bible, they were used by prideful Kings who pillaged the temple of God and worshipped idols to attempt to understand the realm of God, in lieu of the prophets (Daniel 5:7-8). The Word also refers to them as "an observer of times (Deut 18:10)."

Astrology is used most often to give people insights and understanding of the alignment of the planets and stars. Yet, it forgets that God actually created the universe and the real way to understand the universe it to seek God through His Son, Jesus. He will reveal all Truth to you.

Be most careful to avoid horoscopes and any other form of astrology that can open the door for Satan to sneak into your body, and therefore, your life. This form of the spirit of divination is so common that horoscopes are now in the back of most major magazines, in the daily newspaper and all over the internet.

When you find yourself feeling lost and vulnerable, that is when you dig deeper into the things of God. Do not turn to evil methods to try to understand God. You will never find Him in the things of Satan.

Do not turn to evil methods to try to understand God. You will never find Him in the things of Satan.

Fortune tellers/Crystal balls

I could share many stories but the one that sticks out in my mind is me getting a referral from a friend, to a woman named Shante, who did crystal ball readings about twelve years ago. I remember being so excited about meeting with her because it was a time in my life that I was looking for answers and I thought this would give me the insight I needed.

I met her in a dimly lit coffee shop in a part of Seattle called Belltown with dream-catchers, rocks and various other paraphernalia decorating the dark red walls. When I walked in, she was waiting for me with her crystal ball sitting out on the table in a stand. She also had some bird feathers around the base of the crystal ball stand. No one seemed to even notice as they drank their coffee and had their conversations.

She began to tell me that she saw images in the crystal ball and would share with me what they meant. I don't even recall what she saw in her crystal ball, but I do remember feeling like something was very off about it.

The moment I sat with her, I demonstrated to Satan that there was yet another opportunity to sway me from the things of Jesus. No matter how many images you see of fortune tellers in the movies taking actors on great adventures, know that they are not for believers. You have access to the things of God that the world does not.

During the years of my rebellion from Jesus, I searched the various forms of divination, but because I was saved and already belonged to Jesus, His Holy Spirit always let me know that I was way off base.

Good luck charms, pendulums, etc.

To this day, it would not be odd to see a child skipping down the sidewalk singing, "See a penny, pick it up, all day long you'll have good luck." Good luck charms have permeated the pop culture and touched your life in ways you may not even be aware of.

As I read this list of the most common good luck charms, I was surprised at how many of them I had accepted. Ladybugs, rainbows, tigers (considered lucky in Chinese astrology), rabbit's foot (I used to have a pink one on a key chain when I was eight), Buddha figure, dream catchers, horse shoes, nautical star (seen as providing guidance for sailors), four leaf clover/shamrock, wishbone, falling or shooting star, lucky penny, sharks tooth, garlic, and salt, etc.

Even the cross for Christians serves as good luck, a symbol to ward off evil, and protection for the person who bears it. While the cross is a symbol for the believer, it is critical that you do not allow yourself to slip into the belief that a piece of gold or silver can keep you safe. Only God Himself can do this.

I also became familiar with pendulums in my "spiritual" days. I had a friend, Angela, who did pendulum consultations for people. I visited her when I was pregnant because she could use the directions of the pendulum to communicate with my unborn child.

I actually purchased one of her sessions for a friend as a baby shower gift because her baby was in breach position and needed to turn in order to be safely delivered. She was very close to her due date and was open to anything to increase the safety of her unborn child.

It was undeniable that an unforeseen energy was moving the pendulum in response to being asked a question. Yet, it was still a form of the spirit of divination because I was replacing the revelation of God with this symbol. Someone with an extra measure of the gift of discernment can ask the Holy Spirit and He will give the necessary insight that we seek.

Angel Worshiper

Angel worshipers are those who attempt to learn the things of God by trying to make contact with the angels. A commentary I researched best sums up angel worshipping:

God created angels as ministering spirits, but some rebelled at the behest of Satan. However, most remained loyal. God's angels truly bring protection, announcements of great events and warnings before enforcing God's wrath. They are powerful beings who do God's bidding and are never to be worshiped.

Do not let anyone take your crown through false religion, philosophy or the inordinate esteem or worship of angels. – Joe Camarata, *Angel Worship and the First Commandment*

(www.ucg.org/un/uno212)

I think that you must be crystal clear about the different forms of the spirit of divination by now, right? While this is not a comprehensive list, you now have a clear understanding of what the spirit of divination looks like in your life and the lives of others.

Always turn to the Holy Spirit when you need insight from God. Do this through His Word and the Holy Spirit within you. If you are just saved and not born again, ask God for the gift of His Holy Spirit. It is also time for you to walk through the process of hearing His voice that I shared earlier in the book.

DUMB AND DEAF SPIRIT

This is one of the most self-destructive and violent unclean spirits of them all. It is a stronghold spirit that requires unwavering faith and belief by the deliverance minister.

When the disciples could not effectively cast out a dumb and deaf spirit and they inquired why it would not come out at their command, Jesus responded that this spirit can come forth only by prayer and fasting.

> *When Jesus saw that the people came running together, he rebuked the foul spirit, saying unto him, Thou dumb and deaf spirit, I charge thee, come out of him, and enter no more into him.*
>
> *And the spirit cried, and rent him sore, and came out of him: and he was as one dead; insomuch that many said, He is dead.*
>
> *But Jesus took him by the hand, and lifted him up; and he arose. – Matthew 9:25 – 27*

This spirit manifests in many different ways that go far beyond what you would think the words "dumb" and "deaf" refer to in your traditional understanding.

The Fruit of Deaf and Dumb Spirit

- ❐ Inability to speak or express oneself
- ❐ Inner ear disease
- ❐ Insanity
- ☑ Mental illness
- ❐ Epilepsy
- ❐ Convulsions
- ❐ Tearing/Cutting oneself
- ❐ Foaming at the mouth
- ❐ Pining away (motionless stupor)

- ❏ Gnashing/Gritting the teeth
- ☑ Suicidal tendencies
- ❏ Burning oneself
- ❏ Drowning
- ❏ Bruising
- ❏ Blindness
- ❏ Spirit of stupor
- ❏ Madness

How Dumb and Deaf Spirit Enters

As I explored the Word for an explanation of the origin of how dumb and deaf spirit enters, I came to understand that the door first opens when you refuse to pay attention and turn your back on the Lord (Zechariah 7:11). It is also a result of your heart becoming calloused and hardened (Matthew 13:15).

The challenge becomes pinpointing exactly when this turning away from the Lord began because it is passed on from generation to generation.

Inability to speak or express oneself

I know that when I come across someone who cannot seem to express themselves verbally or clearly put their emotions into words, I have come in contact with someone who is carrying the dumb and deaf spirit.

If you feel like your thoughts and feelings get caught in your throat and you just can't seem to get them out, dumb and deaf spirit has found its way into your temple to block your ability to speak clearly.

Inner ear disease

When your ears begin to close from hearing the Lord, it can manifest in actual inner ear disease or the stopping up of your ears.

In the process of the deliverance and healing Jesus was doing through me with Rochelle, a sister of a friend of mine, to remove the unclean fruit of the spirit of infirmity called rheumatoid arthritis, Rochelle began to complain of something being in her ear. Her ear became plugged up and I knew immediately that it was a form of this manifestation of dumb and deaf spirit.

Insanity

Insanity is the void of having a sound mind or temperance (Gal 5:22, 1 Timothy 1:7). I have heard Albert Einstein's definition of insanity as doing the same thing over and over and over while expecting a different outcome. I suppose that doing the same thing over and over again, knowing that it is not getting you anywhere, is not a result of a sound mind. I do know that when you feel insane, you feel like you are coming apart and nothing is connecting correctly. True insanity is when your mind severs from the other aspects of your being.

Mental illness, insanity and madness

Dumb and deaf spirit is responsible for the manifestation of mental illness. Those who were oppressed with this spirit in the Word always suffered mental illness. When this spirit is cast out and the Holy Spirit comes in to repair any damage dumb and deaf spirit caused, they will return to being of sound mind, a fruit of the Holy Spirit.

Epilepsy and foaming at the Mouth

Mark 9:20 records what we have come to know as a possible epileptic seizure.

> *So they brought him. When the spirit saw Jesus, it immediately threw the boy into a convulsion. He fell to the ground and rolled around, foaming at the mouth.*

This is yet another one of the manifestations of this horrible unclean spirit

Convulsions

The violent bodily spasms one experiences during a convulsion are also a result of the occupation of dumb and deaf spirit. There is definitely a pattern of the manifestations of this spirit. It causes loss of mental and physical facilities and control. This also includes tearing and cutting yourself and/or gnashing or the gritting of your teeth.

Pining away and spirit of stupor

This spirit can also manifest in a completely opposite fashion by creating what the Word calls "pining away (Mark 9:18)." It is a motionless stupor that creates a blank look with no motion. It is as if they are sedated with heavy drugs. Romans 11:8 describes the spirit of stupor as having eyes that cannot see and ears that cannot hear. I also listed this spirit with the spirit of bondage because it can also be a result of the presence of that spirit.

Suicidal tendencies

If you are, or have ever been oppressed with this spirit, it caused you to have thoughts of suicide. It teams with lying spirit to almost convince you that your life is not worth living and if you took your own life, no one would notice.

It causes you to inflict bodily harm on yourself and possibly even causes you to attempt to take your own life. By the fact that you are reading this book, God kept you and made sure that you were here to complete the work He created in you. You can be free from this for the rest of your life, just keep reading on. These suicidal tendencies can also manifest in burning and bruising yourself, or making attempts at drowning yourself.

Blindness

The Word also draws a connection to blindness as a demonstration of dumb and deaf spirit.

> *Then they brought him a demon-possessed man who was blind and mute, and Jesus healed him, so that he could both talk and see. – Matthew 12:22*

At this point you may be like one of the women at a retreat at which I was ministering and sharing some of these unclean fruit. Afterward, she replied, "Good grief! Boy am I messed up!" Don't feel bad. We are all struggling with the unclean in our walk with God. And I'm not even done yet. There are even fouler spirits that may have inhabited your life that you need to get rid of. Let's move on to spirit of jealousy.

SPIRIT OF JEALOUSY

There are two types of jealousy mentioned in scripture. One means "jealousy," and one means "envy." When God says He is a jealous God (Exodus 20:50) and his name is Jealous, (Joshua 24:19), it means that you are His possession and He allows nothing to fill the void He created within you that only He can fill. This is not the form of jealousy that this section talks about.

There is also envy and that is to covet something that does not belong to you. Envy is defined as discontent aroused by another's better fortune, etc. You may think of scorned lovers when you think of jealousy, but it is much more serious in the many ways it can be demonstrated in your life.

Here is the evidence of the spirit of jealousy in your life:

The Fruit of the Spirit of Jealousy

- ☑ Violence/Murder TV shows
- ☑ Anger/Rage
- ☐ Creates division
- ☐ Wrath
- ☑ Revenge
- ☑ Spite
- ☐ Hate
- ☐ Cruelty
- ☑ Suspicion
- ☐ Coveting
- ☐ Competition
- ☐ Emulation

How The Spirit of Jealousy Enters

The spirit of jealousy usually enters into the life of a child when he or she experiences their parent or parents showing preferential treatment to another sibling. I have noticed that it is also present in children who experienced a parent leaving through divorce, separation or abandonment. Then, when the parent starts another family or has step-children, he or she may perceive that the children of the second family are treated better and are more loved.

Violence/Murder

When I first saw this topic listed as an unclean spirit, I was deeply struck at the power that we have at our fingertips to transform the world. We have become a society where violence and murder is common. One does not have to linger long in front of the television to confirm this.

Violence and murder are frequent and you must be careful to protect what you allow into your mind and the minds of your children by what you spend time watching. I stopped turning on the evening news. When I used to watch it, my daughter would always call out from upstairs, "Mommy, whatever you are watching is making me feel bad." She would experience certain feelings based on certain shows that were on. At first I thought perhaps she can just hear the television and I had the volume up too loud. No. She could literally *feel* that something wasn't right in the energy of the house.

Before I was cleaned, I could sit and watch shows like Law & Order, Law & Order Special Victims Unit, Crime Scene Investigation (until it just became too graphic), Criminal Minds and The Closer (that used to be my favorite). And let me not forget the evening news. Now, I cannot stand to even have any shows about murder and violence on at all in my presence.

Even television shows on violence and murder can open doors for unclean spirits to enter into your life. As soon as I stopped allowing those shows in my house, the energy literally felt different and lighter.

This may be tough for you to hear because violent shows literally create an addictive-type following that you may be experiencing. I was doing some deliverance work on a client's husband in leading her in casting down the spirits he was dealing with. During one conversation she was talking about how he just comes home from work and watches TV for hours. I knew that he was dealing with the spirit of jealousy and the spirit of bondage, so he was drawn to shows that were all about violence and murder. Like spirits draw like spirits.

Anger and rage

Even though you may have heard someone refer to anger or rage as spirits, they are actually fruits of the spirit of jealousy. When you experience anger, it is usually in response to a situation in which you feel that someone else is being treated better or differently and you do not feel honored. Whatever the reason for you experiencing anger, in order to get rid of it for more than a season, you must cast out the spirit of jealousy that manifests in anger and rage.

Creates division

Far too many believers in churches constantly create division among church members, leadership, ministries, and anywhere else in which they can gain access. Those who are carrying this spirit can almost single-handedly keep tension among family members that leads to division and separation. That is their mission and more times than not, they are successful in achieving their mission until you realize that it is a spiritual issue and can be put to an end.

Wrath

Wrath is a little trickier than anger and rage to identify because it lies dormant and is easily disguised. Because it is extreme anger, it usually hides until certain "buttons" are pushed. I have seen wrath from many people in the church, including a first lady.

She was one of the most beautiful, sweet, and humorous people I knew...until you became the target of her wrath. All of a sudden, her tongue would become sharp and you had no idea what was going to come out of her mouth. She would send her amour-bearers to various people in the congregation to send them to her so she could "rebuke" them. Rebuke is a form of love and there was no love there, only wrath. I used to joke to myself not to get in her way because I would feel her wrath. The Word speaks of the wrath of God, and any wrath other than His should not be tolerated.

Revenge

When you feel the need to seek revenge, it is the operation of this unclean fruit. I have seen many, many examples of this spirit in both men and women. I have probably seen the most twisted cases with scorned women. I have seen them cut tires, scratch the paint job on cars, call uncontrollably, fight, and plot some of the most sinister plots to get "the other woman."

I'm sure you can think of many examples of revenge with your friends, family, and acquaintances. However crazy the stories may seem, it is the urging of this wicked spirit. Scripture reminds us:

> *Dearly beloved, avenge not yourselves, but rather give place unto wrath: for it is written, Vengeance is mine; I will repay, saith the Lord. – Romans 12:19 KJ*

Spite and hate

If you hold grudges against people and feel any bitterness in your heart, than you are aware of what spite is. It is a close relative of revenge and not a normal result of being hurt. You really can go through hurt without spite and hardened feelings of ill will. Unresolved spite turns into hate and cruelty.

Cruelty

Have you ever met someone who is just cruel? Most cruel people actually enjoy torturing, tormenting, and manipulating people with threats of harm and violence. Cruelty is deliberately causing pain and suffering and it is an aspect of the fruit of jealousy.

Suspicion

The presence of the spirit of jealousy creates distrust and the assumption that people have bad intentions and are guilty of something. This is not the same as the Holy Spirit showing you that something is wrong. Suspicion is looking for something that does not exist out of insecurity and taking it as real.

Coveting and emulation

This is something that I see running rampant in today's church. We covet people's callings, gifts, talents, spouses, friends, cars, houses, clothing, knowledge, and titles. You can even easily look at the first couple of the church and want whatever their relationship appears to be.

I also see it in the business world, especially in network marketing companies, where you have been taught to duplicate others' success, assuming that you will then have the same success. When I was involved in network marketing, I always heard my up line say, "Do what I've done and you'll get what I've got." It does not work that way because God created you with different gifts, purpose and calling than him or her. That up line was chosen for that success and you may not have been. This unclean fruit festers and evolves into competition.

Competition

The most notorious case of competition in the Word is the story of Cain and Abel (Genesis 4:5-8). You must get in your spirit that there is no competition in God. In God's Kingdom, we all have a purpose and there is more than enough for all of us. You don't ever have to compete because God created you for a specific purpose. The way He will have you do something is different than anyone else on the planet.

We're almost done with the strongholds and must move on to the final two so you can learn how to remove these strongholds. The great news is that any of these manifestations will also leave your life as you cast out the stronghold spirits.

ANTICHRIST SPIRIT

I received an email from a man who was clearly oppressed by the antichrist spirit. I could even tell over email with no live interaction. I knew in my spirit that he not only had perverse spirit living in him, but also the antichrist spirit.

The moment he came at me with such opposition, I sensed the presence of many unclean spirits. One of the most prominent ones was the antichrist. He was enraged at the things of Jesus and the people who carry His message. The Word is clear in identifying when someone is carrying the antichrist spirit.

> *This is how you can recognize the Spirit of God: Every spirit that acknowledges that Jesus Christ has come in the flesh is from God, 3but every spirit that does not acknowledge Jesus is not from God. This is the spirit of the antichrist, which you have heard is coming and even now is already in the world.*
>
> *You, dear children, are from God and have overcome them, because the one who is in you is greater than the one who is in the world. They are from the world and therefore speak from the viewpoint of the world, and the world listens to them. We are from God, and whoever knows God listens to us; but whoever is not from God does not listen to us. This is how we recognize the Spirit of truth and the spirit of falsehood. – 1 John 4:2-6*
>
> *Many deceivers, who do not acknowledge Jesus Christ as coming in the flesh, have gone out into the world. Any such person is the deceiver and the antichrist. – 2 John 1:7*

The Fruit of Antichrist Spirit

- ❐ Against/Opposes Christ
- ❐ Refuses to repent

❏ Claims authority other than Christ
❏ Opposes prophecy
❏ Blasphemies against the gifts
❏ Persecutes believers
❏ Seeks to take over and control others
❏ Suppresses ministries
❏ Vexes a righteous soul
❏ Tries to seduce into error
❏ Seduces people into worshipping them and not God
❏ Spirit of falsehood
❏

Again, there are so many possible ways antichrist spirit can show up and the Word is so straightforward on this unclean spirit that I did not go into detail with this list. The easiest way to identify the antichrist spirit is anyone who comes against Jesus or the Holy Spirit. It often goes hand-in-hand with the spirit of divination as people seek the things of God through means other than Jesus or His Holy Spirit.

I think you've got it. At this point, I also run the risk of boring you beyond return. One more and we're done.

SPIRIT OF INFIRMITY

If you have forgotten your power over sickness and death through Jesus, then this section may shake you up a bit. There is an overwhelming amount of sickness in the Body of Christ. Sickness is not of God. The Holy Spirit carries the healing power of God. Because many churches are not moving in the fullness of the Holy Spirit and therefore believers are not experiencing supernatural healing of God as they should.

Recently, I was watching a DVD of a faith healer, Thurman Scrivner (www.tlsm.org), and he was moving in the Absolute Truth. He boldly stated that "No Christians should ever be sick or have diseases." Yet, we see sick Christians in every church on every street corner. Where did we get separated from the Truth that we are healed through Jesus Christ? The Truth is that all sickness and disease is a result of the presence of the spirit of infirmity.

If your faith has been waning in this area, my prayer is that this section will help re-align you with the Truth of the healing to which you have full access. This list should be much, much longer and include every sickness and disease known to man. No matter the name of the sickness or disease, you have been granted the authority, power and dominion to be healed from it.

It has become normal for Christians to be sick and diseased. It is time for this to stop. Enough. Too many of us have buried our God-fearing loved ones due to sickness and disease. From this instant forward you have to know that you have been given the power to heal through Jesus.

The Fruit of the Spirit of Infirmity

- ❏ Colds
- ❏ Fevers
- ❏ Virus infections

- ☐ Fungus
- ☐ Bloody flux
- ☐ Asthma
- ☐ Sinus issues
- ☐ Hay fever
- ☐ Arthritis
- ☐ Frailty (impotent, weak, feeble)
- ☐ Malady
- ☐ Pain
- ☐ Diseases of all types
- ☐ Sickness of all types

How Spirit of Infirmity Enters

This stronghold mainly enters through a lack of knowing and believing the Word of God and failing to stand on it with unshakeable faith. It can also enter when other strongholds are present to "open the door." The spirit of infirmity is often passed down through generations.

As I type these words, I am reminded of one of the first things a doctor's office asks you when you step into their office – your family history. Even the secular world understands that if you have had sickness and disease in your family, that it is passed down from generation to generation.

I am not going to explain any of its manifestations as they are all self-explanatory and too numerous. Just know that every single form of sickness and disease is a result of the presence of the spirit of infirmity. It is the presence of the spirit of infirmity that causes the body to manifest disease when you do not realize that as the temple of God, you are to be free from disease and sickness. (Take a d-e-e-p breath).

> *Every single form of sickness and disease is a result of the presence of the spirit of infirmity.*

The reason I actually began to study deliverance was in order to move into the fullness of my calling as a healer. I first had to understand deliverance. What I did not expect is that the very act of being delivered creates healing. When the spirit responsible for the appearance of a sickness is expelled, the sickness and its symptoms leave with it.

You were designed to be healthy. Being free of all sickness and disease is part of your divine inheritance from Jesus. By His stripes, you are healed.

This is the topic of my next book, but for now all you need to know is that deliverance is a prerequisite for healing. Once the spirit of infirmity has been commanded out of your temple, it is important to call in the Holy Spirit to heal any damage that unclean spirits have left behind.

Where Do You Go From Here?

If you are like me when I first read through these unclean fruits, I was like "My goodness, I am MESSED up!" I was absolutely blown away to know that much of what my life had become at the time was an amalgamation of the fruit of unclean spirits. I was even more amazed to think of the thousands of hours I have spent over the last eight years coaching people was actually only teaching them how to manage their unclean fruit.

God left us a clear path to rid ourselves of each and every one of the unclean fruit that have knowingly and unknowingly found themselves in our lives (Hallelujah!). Now that you know what unclean fruit you have been carrying and which stronghold spirits are responsible for them, it is time to dismiss them from your life once and for all.

Remember that every stronghold spirit and its fruit is subject to the name of Jesus. You no longer have to live with any of these issues plaguing your life. Jesus came so you would have a way out. Be encouraged that the old is about to fall away so you can become the person God created you to be – free and free, indeed.

Read on and I will explain exactly how they are expelled and what to expect in this process.

DAILY PRAYER OF PROTECTION AND POWER

Heavenly Father, in the name of Jesus, I bow in worship and praise before you. The blood of the Lord Jesus Christ covers me as my protection during this time of prayer. I surrender myself completely and unreservedly in every area of my life to you. I stand in the full power, authority and dominion over all things of the spiritual realm and of the natural realm through Jesus Christ, My Lord and Savior.

In the name of Jesus, He stands against all the workings of Satan that would hinder me in this time of prayer, and I address myself only to the true and living God. I stand in the fullness of knowing that The Kingdom of God is within me and I am a living temple fully committed to Jesus.

Heavenly Father, you are worthy to receive all the glory and honor and praise. I renew my allegiance to you and pray that the blessed Holy Spirit would enable me in this time of prayer. I am thankful, Heavenly Father, that you have loved me and sent the Lord Jesus Christ into the world to die as my substitute, that I would be redeemed.

Father in the name of Jesus, I ask for forgiveness for any sins I have committed both knowingly or unknowingly and for each and every time I have fallen short of your glory. I am thankful that through Him, you have completely forgiven me; you have given me eternal life; you have given me the perfect righteousness of the Lord Jesus Christ, so I am now justified. I am thankful that in Him you have made me complete, and that you have offered yourself to me to be my strength, joy and center of my life.

Jesus, come and open my eyes that I might see how great you are and how complete your provision is for this new day. I do, in the name of my Lord and Savior Jesus Christ, take my place with Christ in the heavenlies with all principalities and powers under my feet.

I am thankful for the victory the Lord Jesus Christ won for me on the Cross and His resurrection has been given to me and that I am now seated with the Lord Jesus Christ in the heavenlies; therefore, I declare that all principalities and powers and all wicked spirits are subject to me in the name of the Lord Jesus Christ.

I am thankful for the armor you have provided, and I put on the girdle of truth, the breastplate of righteousness, the sandals of peace, the helmet of salvation. I lift up the shield of faith against all the fiery darts of the Enemy, and take in my hand the sword of the Spirit, the Word of God, and use your Word against all the forces of evil in my life; and I put on this armor and live and pray in complete dependence upon you, blessed Holy Spirit.

I claim the victory in my life today. I affirm that the Word of God is true and whatsoever I speak will come to pass. Your Word says that whatever I bind on earth is bound in heaven, and whatever I loose on earth is loosed in heaven. I choose to live today in the light of God's Word. I choose, Jesus, to live in obedience and fellowship with you.

I stand firmly planted in the certainty of faith that through my Heavenly Father, I have the power to give life to the dead and call things that are not as though they were. By faith and in dependence upon you, I put off the old man and stand in all the victory and provision Jesus made for me there to live above sin.

I put off the old nature with its selfishness, and I put on the new nature with its love. I put off the old nature with its fear and I put on the new nature with its power. I put off the old nature with its weakness and all its deceitful lusts and I put on the new nature with all its righteousness and purity.

Blessed Holy Spirit, I welcome you and pray that you will fill me. I am thankful that you have made provision so that today I can live filled with the Spirit of God with love, joy and self-control in my life. I surrender myself to you, Lord Jesus Christ, as a living sacrifice. I give my will and my body to you, recognizing that I am your temple; and I rejoice in your mercy and your goodness.

I choose not to be conformed to this world. I choose to be transformed by the renewing of my mind and I pray that you would show me your will and enable me to walk in all the fullness of the will of God today. I choose to think my thoughts after you and be of power, love and a sound mind. Today, I decree that all the forces of the spiritual and natural realm line up in perfect harmony with the fullness of God's purpose and calling on my life.

I declare that I believe in miracles and have dedicated every aspect of my mind, body, spirit, soul and life to Jesus as Holy Ground. God, I ask that you manifest miracles in my life today and that what is impossible with me becomes possible with you. I believe in miracles and the power of Jesus to do the impossible. - In Jesus' Name, Amen.

This prayer is adapted from Mark Bubeck's book The Adversary (Chicago: Moody Press, 1975) and was written by Dr. Victor Matthews and lightly edited by Dr. Neil T. Anderson. Printed in The Handbook for Spiritual Warfare by Dr. Ed Murphy (Nashville, Thomas Nelson Publishers, Inc., 1992,1996)

Chapter Nine

Casting Out The Unclean

It is time for you to be free. Now that you are clear about which unclean spirits have moved into your temple, they must be cast out. It is not enough to be aware of them. They have to get out so you can be about your Father's business.

Make sure that you have done (and not just read through) each and every exercise in *Chapter Six: Is Your Heart Ready For God*? DO NOT proceed to any of the work of casting out spirits if you do not sincerely feel like you have released any and all unforgiveness from your heart. You may need to go through the steps in Chapter Six again, until you get the go-ahead from the Holy Spirit. He will guide and lead you by letting you know when you are ready. Just move quietly and listen to God's instructions. Proceed only when you have been released to do so.

If you are still questioning the truth of this work, you are not ready. Do not proceed to see *if* it works, you must be certain. Curiosity does not count.

If you are not certain of your heavenly rank through Christ Jesus, go back to Chapter Three: *Remembering Who You Are* and explore the scriptures that are listed throughout the chapter. You must be certain of your power and Heavenly position so all of Heaven and earth knows who you are. Also make sure you set aside time to study the scriptures listed in the Scripture References in the back of the book.

Are you certain?

Preparing For The Process

Once you have completed the steps to forgiveness and understand which fruits of unclean spirits you have been carrying, then you have to create the correct atmosphere for your deliverance. The first step is to read through the rest of the book before you move into deliverance, so you completely comprehend the full experience.

Once the devil has entered into your temple and life, there are five things that have to be in place in order to get him out:

The Absolute Truth of God

Belief

Forgiveness

Reconnection and realignment your mind, spirit and body with the mind of Jesus, and

Casting him and his unclean spirits out.

Without all five ingredients present at the time of deliverance, you will only get partial results or no results at all. You not only need the Absolute Truth of God, belief in the Word of God, and forgiveness, you must be fully connected in your spirit, heart and soul. Then, they obey when they are cast out.

Breaking The Unclean Ties

Take a look back at the fruits or manifestations you are experiencing in your life. You can impact these unclean spirits immediately by closing any doors to iniquity and sin in your life.

In other words, cease any and all unclean behavior in which you are still engaged. I don't mean get ready to stop; I mean stop it – now. This will begin to break the access that you have provided to Satan. If you have been fornicating, now that you know that it has opened the door to stronghold spirits, you must decide to stop today.

Whatever behavior that you have been participating in as identified in the previous checklists must stop today. Throw away any vices, books, tools, toys, pictures, or symbols that have served as doorways. I know that this will not be easy because the very spirit that is drawing you to the behavior has not left your temple yet.

Today is the day that you move to a new realm in your relationship with God. Now that you know how, you have no more excuses standing between you and the life you desire.

What To Expect When They Come Out

Even today as I sit down to write, I was in church service as the Pastor was bringing a particularly cutting message about how we can lose Christ right in the church if we are not careful. I noticed that at the times when he was sharing the deep truth of the scripture, there were many, many coughs coming from the congregation.

One woman began coughing so violently that she got up and left the sanctuary. I knew that it was Truth getting down into the spirits of people and literally causing them to cough out unclean spirits. The sad part was that no one understood this work and therefore opportunities to further deliver people were missed. We must understand this piece of the work of Jesus if we are to complete the work He began in delivering His believers.

The unclean spirits are residing within you and because they have been there awhile, they set up an order of governance. It reminds me of the *Mucinex* commercial that shows a family of annoying mucus that have set up residence inside the chest cavity of the sick person. When the medicine hits, they are coughed out and expelled.

That is exactly how it works with unclean spirits. They have moved in, become comfortable and have gone rather undetected up to this point. Because they use your body to hear and see (Satan is the prince of the air), they are well aware of the fact that you have gotten this book and they are about to be evicted.

They try to stir up as much as they can so you don't go through with the process of kicking them out. They know that you belong to Jesus, so all they can do is squat until you understand the process of getting them out once and for all. They will not go until they are directly commanded out.

Hollywood movie making has truly messed up the concept of unclean spirits being expelled. I had one older, more conservative client who thought her head might turn in a 360 degree circle, thanks to the movie, *Exorcist*. I don't want to disappoint you, but it is not Hollywood at all.

It was the book, *Pigs in the Parlor* that shared what the process of an unclean spirit being expelled looks like. The books shared that because the Holy Spirit is always associated with breath, unclean spirits are expelled through the nose and mouth. I have found it absolutely true. Hear me in this...there is always outward evidence of unclean spirits being expelled.

There is always evidence of unclean spirits being expelled.

You will always experience deep exhales, yawns, coughing, and often coughing that is so uncontrollable that it leads to gagging and may cause you to cough up a slime-like substance.

While I have heard it described as vomiting, it is actually not the regurgitation of previously ingested food or drink. Yes, I know, it sounds gross, but I have to take you there in order for this work to be complete.

I have also seen sneezing, tearing eyes and runny noses as evidence that an unclean spirit is being expelled. I have heard people being delivered describe a foul taste in their mouths and strange feelings in their bodies as their unclean spirits were on the way out. There was one instance in which unclean spirits came out burping (imagine my surprise as this was going on). At one point during this deliverance, both the client and I cracked up because she is such a polite person by nature and it was something to hear these huge, long burps coming from her.

Remember that if you are attending a deliverance service at a church, no matter how exciting and emotion-filled it may be, unless there is an outward manifestation of the unclean spirit leaving, it is still living within you. This is one of the pieces of this work that we have missed in the church and the Body of Christ.

Unless there is an outward manifestation of the unclean spirit leaving, it is still living within you.

The Holy Spirit's Role

The most critical thing that must be present in order to proceed is that you must have the ability to hear and recognize the voice of the Holy Spirit. You can only do your own deliverance or someone else's if you can see and hear from the Holy Spirit to lead and guide your every step.

This sounds like it may be easy, but the presence of unclean spirits affect your ability to see and hear God. Be honest with yourself. If you are not actively hearing from God daily, you will need to seek out someone else to walk you through the casting out of the spirits.

As soon as I complete this book, I will be creating a training program for ministers to be fully trained in this deliverance process. If you don't know of anyone who can walk you through this work, you can contact your church, a local church that moves in deliverance, or my ministry (see back of book for more info).

No matter how willing I am to be a vessel for this work, it is not mine. It is the Holy Spirit using me. There is not a simple cookie-cutter approach that works on everyone because the orientation of your unclean spirits is different from anyone else's.

It is the Holy Spirit that will give you the glimpse you need to see of how they have grown attached to each other. When I am doing deliverance, the Holy Spirit shows me how the unclean spirits have attached to one another and which ones are the dominant spirits. The Holy Spirit also allows me to hear the spirits and feel what is going on inside the body of the person who is being delivered. I could not do this work without the Holy Spirit.

Because the Holy Spirit gives access to this work to every believer, the same should be true for you. With your new understanding and God leading the way, you may be able to deliver others. But, make sure you have been cleansed in your heart and spirit and have received confirmation from the Holy Spirit that you are clean before you attempt to deliver anyone else. You will be very clear in the difference you will feel once you are cleaned or delivered. If you are not feeling a huge difference from how you felt before, then you have not been fully cleansed and delivered.

God will always send confirmation and you will be tested in your cleanliness. You should find that you respond differently than you did before. For instance, if you were carrying anger that

Confirmation of deliverance

the spirit of jealousy created in you, once you are delivered, the same people and things will not make you angry. Your reaction will be transformed. You will know when you are delivered.

Making The Connection

God held up this book's entrance into the world so I could share this portion of the work with you. As I was recently doing a deliverance session, nothing was happening. I mean nothing. I was working with two people simultaneously and no matter how many people are participating, when deliverance is occurring it is physically evident and leaves no question as to its effectiveness. The Holy Spirit allowed me to feel their spirit from the inside-out and the only two words I could use to describe what I felt were "empty" and "deadness."

I left that session feeling baffled and sought God on understanding what was happening. I literally felt a complete detachment of their mind, body, spirit and soul. The Holy Spirit began to show me that their family circumstances left them emotionally traumatized.

One of them had tried just about everything from counseling, prayer, having hands laid on him and seeking deliverance. Over the years, nothing was effectively sustained. He had grown weary of even trying. The other participant was dealing with mental illness and intense emotional bitterness at her father for being verbally abusive and not being present for her throughout her life.

Then, the Holy Spirit began to show me what was happening. He showed me that He allows this disconnection to occur in those who are emotionally or physically traumatized so they can survive their day-to-day lives. They literally become detached and they feel disconnected from the world, God, and the Holy Spirit inside of them. They literally are depending solely on their human spirit to survive. It is like they are placed within a cocoon, so they can continue making it day-to-day. He also showed me that the same thing happens to people who are dealing with physical illness, disabilities and chronic diseases.

But I still did not understand how to proceed with their deliverance as they were living with this disconnection. I knew that deliverance would not work until they were first "re-connected." I asked the Holy Spirit, "What do I need to do to reconnect them?"

As I was waiting on God to answer my question about the process of reconnecting, He began to show me just how prevalent this problem is within the Body of Christ. He also showed me that there are countless people who are unable to experience deliverance and healing because they have become severed from God. He showed me a pipe that has been broken off into several pieces and is no longer in one piece so things can flow through their body temples properly.

Shortly thereafter, He brought the answer. It was one of those rare moments that somehow without any doing of my own, my favorite old, tattered Bible I received from my childhood church in 1988, was opened to the very scripture God was trying to show me. I was sitting on the edge of my bed and heard God say, "Command." When I first heard the word, "command," I thought in my spirit, "Command? I hear You, Lord, but *how* do I do that."

Then, I looked down and saw the answer in the Word. It was opened to Hebrews 11:1 and the all-familiar scripture, "*Now faith is being sure of what we hope for and certain of what we do not see. This is what the ancients were commended for.*" And then the next words lifted off of the page, "*By faith we understand that the universe was formed at God's command, so that what is seen was not made out of what was visible.*" The word, "command" nearly illuminated to make sure I did not miss it.

Command. Then He showed me a vision of Him forming the earth from nothingness with the power of His Word. I knew that when the Holy Spirit told me to "command," He was instructing me to speak and command their connection in His name and it would obey my spoken command. He then showed me the same image of the pipe, but this time the pieces were moving into place in response to the words I spoke.

In our next session, I explained what the Holy Spirit had shown me and assigned them the homework of commanding their mind, body, spirit, and soul to line up with the Holy Spirit within them. In my next session with one of the participants, I was amazed to literally feel that he had "reconnected."

If you are reading this section and know that this speaks to how you have been feeling within, then you must first do the work of commanding the pieces of who you are to reconnect before you can proceed with the work of deliverance. I praise God for holding up this work to ensure that I was able to explain this important and misunderstood aspect of the deliverance process.

Speaking To Unclean Spirits

As I mentioned earlier, you must speak directly to the unclean spirits. Jesus has already given you the authority over them and requires that you stand in that authority. Make sure you are not asking God to deal with the spirits for you. He does not respond because He already gave you the authority to do this work in Jesus' name.

> Make sure you are not asking God to deal with
> the spirits for you. He does not respond because
> He already gave you the authority to do this
> work in Jesus' name.

When I first talked to Apostle Forte about exactly how to expel unclean spirits, he reminded me that I have to speak to them like they are unruly and mischievous children. You do not ask little Suzy to pick up her mess with a high-pitched voice that sounds like a question. You boldly put some power in your voice and insist, "Susy, clean up this mess!" The same is true as you deal with unclean spirits.

You must be very specific about what they can and cannot do. They will find a way to get into any and everything you do not say is off limits. You will see what I mean when you read the prayers and commands that are at the end of this chapter. Unclean spirits respond just like little Johnny responds when you say to him, "Johnny, pick up your socks off of the stairs." Even though there may be socks, a video game and a baseball cap, he will only pick up the socks. Then you look at him and say, "Johnny, why didn't you pick up your game and baseball cap and put those away, too?" He'll reply, "Mom! You only said to pick up the socks."

Don't leave a stone unturned when you are dealing with the unclean.

Identifying the "Lid" Spirit

Remember when I used the analogy of the little mucus family in the *Mucinex* commercial? The unclean spirits set up shop inside your body just like the little mucus creatures in the commercial. Not only do they set up shop, they create a hierarchy or little invisible governance system. One unclean spirit "rules" and has the most influence over the others. In order to get all of the unclean spirits out, you must first recognize the governing, or what I call the "lid" spirit. Once you identify and cast out the lid spirit, the others will come out.

You can attempt to cast out the spirits that are not the lid spirit and you will only get minimal results if any at all. As I was learning this, I shared it with my dear friend Martha, who attends a church where the pastor moves heavily in deliverance. She said that he had just taught that fact in their Bible study lesson. He shared how in the Word that Jesus first had to identify the governing or "lid" spirit, cast it out and then proceed to cast out the remaining unclean spirits (Luke 8:28 – 39 KJ)

If you are unable to identify the "lid" spirit, just as Jesus did in this same passage of scripture, you can ask the name or the nature of the unclean spirit and they must let you know their name. Every time I have had it identify itself, the spirit has either given me its name by speaking it through the client, I have heard it in my spirit or the client hears it directly from the Holy Spirit.

Once I know the name of the governing unclean spirit, I can then command it to leave and never return again. Refer to the command at the end of the chapter for an example of what to say when speaking to Satan and his unclean spirits.

Following the Eviction *Rest*

Once the unclean spirits have been expelled, you will feel somewhat like a wet noodle – emptied out. The other feeling I often hear is a deep sense of peace and then wanting to rest. Your body needs to do what I call, "recalibrate." It needs to regenerate the cells of the body without the unclean spiritual matter and, detox your system. You need to rest and sleep to support your temple in completing this work. You may feel tired for a few days following your deliverance. This is to be expected.

Now that you have been cleansed, the last step to the process is being filled with the clean spirits and their fruit so you can be whole and complete. You cannot be left empty and without the proper clean spirits to operate fully in your calling and purpose. You're not there quite yet... read on through Chapter Ten for the last part of this process.

INTRODUCTORY PRAYER AND COMMAND

I use a similar prayer to this one, or as the Holy Spirit moves me at the beginning of a deliverance session. I move directly from the prayer to the declaration and command, without a break in the process. I included these so you can get the feel for just how authoritatively you must speak to unclean spirits and how to close every door through which they have gained access.

Heavenly Father, in the name of Jesus, I thank you and praising you for being such an awesome and mighty God. Thank you for your power, Thank you for your wisdom. Thank you for making me the head and not the tail and openly and lovingly providing the keys to your Kingdom so I can live life and life more abundantly, in Jesus' name.

Lord, I am humbled by the power of your Word and I present my body and my life as a living sacrifice to your will and your way. I come standing on your Word as the Truth and your will for my life. Lord, your Word says that you will sprinkle clean water on me and save me from my uncleanliness.

Father, in the name of Jesus, now that I am clean, call for the grain, make it plentiful and do not allow famine to overtake my life. You said that you will increase the fruit of the trees and the crops of the field. Thank you in advance for this Word coming to pass in my life.

Father God, I Thank you for leaving me a clear path to living out the fullness of your will. Thank you that through you, Lord Jesus, the works of Satan have been destroyed and I can live above sin. Lord, thank you for the deliverance and the breaking of every stronghold in my life.

In the name of Jesus, from this day forward I walk in the fullness of your will with no obstacles or hindrances in the way. I stand on your word that tells me that you will do what I ask in your name. I ask that every unclean spirit is removed from me today. I ask that every place they have left void be filled with your Holy Spirit. I ask that any damage that the unclean spirits have caused in my temple will be reversed, restored and rejuvenated.

Thank you for your Word that grants me the authority to cause one-thousand demons to flee in your name. This will be a fast work and this work will be complete this day, in the name of Jesus.

Today, I am restored to my rightful position at the right hand of Jesus and I commit myself to doing even greater works that you have left for me to do. Guide me through this process and clearly identify the names of the unclean spirits and how they have oriented themselves in my temple.

Lord, open my spiritual eyes so that I may see you. Open my spiritual ears so that I may hear you as I move forward in your work. Your Word says that what is impossible with man is possible with you. Nothing is impossible for you. I declare that I believe in you and the power of your name as the God of miracles. I ask for a miraculous deliverance right now and consider it done in Jesus' name, Amen.

DECLARATION OF DOMINION AND AUTHORITY

The first thing I do is reestablish the authority Jesus has granted me through His name. Here is an example command for you.

Father, in the name of Jesus, I decree and declare that I belong to Jesus, the name above all names and the name to which every unclean thing must bow and obey. My spirit, mind, body, and soul all belong to my Lord and Savior Jesus Christ who is the master of my life. I am his precious possession and stand in all of the power, dominion and authority that is in His name.

Today, in Jesus' name, I receive the inheritance as a co-heir with Christ to all of the good and abundance that God has for me. I receive every blessing and miracle that God has set aside especially for me.

I am a child of the Most High God and before Him there is no other God. I cast down any idols in my life that I am aware of or that I am not aware of. I confess that I have fallen short of your glory and ask for your forgiveness now, in the name of Jesus'. I turn away from any behavior or choices I have made that do not reflect the glory of my Father Jesus.

I declare that I fully understand and believe that I sit at the right hand of Jesus in the heavenly rank and therefore stand in all of the power and authority that this spiritual rank affords me, in Jesus' name, Amen.

COMMANDING THE UNCLEAN

After I establish the authority, the next step is to establish the boundaries for the unclean spirits. You have to be very specific.

In the name of Jesus, as I stand in the power, authority and dominion that you have provided me. I declare that I am Holy Ground. I belong to Jesus and my body is His temple. Satan, you have no jurisdiction on Holy Ground. In the name of Jesus, you have no rights, no authority, no power and no will to operate any longer in my life. I am now fully aware of your deceptive ways and they end today, in the name of Jesus.

My Master Jesus Christ defeated your master Satan, therefore, you are subject to the name of Jesus and must obey the words that are spoken. In the name of Jesus, every unclean spirit and the fruit that it has attempted to grow in my temple and life must leave today the instant you are commanded to leave. You must take with you any other unclean spirits and you are never to return again. You will go where the Words says you are to go – into the dry and arid place and you are never allowed to enter into any living or unloving thing forever, in Jesus' name.

No matter how long you have been in my temple and no matter how you got in, you will get out and you will stay out of my temple forever. You are not allowed to come near my family, my loved ones, my home, my work place, my church or any other place that my feet touch from this day forward.

You are not allowed to manifest in anyone I come in contact with from this day forward in Jesus' name.

In the name of Jesus, you are not allowed to manifest any of my belongings or anything at all in my life or the lives of anyone I come in contact with from this day forward. I now declare everything I touch, everything God has blessed me with and everyone I cross paths with as Holy Ground and you are not allowed in Holy Ground in Jesus' name.

From this instant forward, no unclean spirit is allowed to even speak my name through anyone else's mouth. Their lips are sealed and they cannot utter my name in any negative way from this day forward.

In the name of Jesus, every unclean spirit that is called by name and those that are not called by name must immediately come up and come out, in Jesus' name. You are to detach yourselves from one another and any other part of my body, mind, spirit and soul. In the name of Jesus, line up one-by-one and without hesitation, you will obey the commands. You have no rights, you have no will and you are not allowed to hesitate or attempt to influence any other unclean spirits in this process. Your time is up and this temple is returning one-hundred percent to Jesus.

I belong to Jesus and from this instant forward, in His name, you will never stop or slow me down again from doing the will of God. You have tried and it has not worked. I am more committed to living out the will of my Lord and Savior than ever before. In Jesus' name, you are powerless against the righteousness in which I live. You will no longer affect my life in anyway. Every door that I am aware of and those that I am not aware of it now shut and you have no access to my life. Every named or unnamed unclean spirit and its fruit must come out when commanded, in the name of Jesus.

You are no longer allowed to wreak havoc on my life and every door of access is now closed. Every generational door is now closed. Every door that was opened in any way in my life is now closed. Any door that anyone else opened in my life is

*now closed to you and you have no more access to me in any
way, shape or form, in Jesus' name. All this we ask, in the
mighty name of Jesus. Amen.*

Then, beginning with the lid spirit, speak to each spirit and
its fruit. Remember that you should not speak the word, "I," such
as, "In the name of Jesus, spirit of fear, I command you to come
out." This is ineffective because Satan is not subject to you, He is
subject to Jesus. Here is an example for you:

> *In the name of Jesus, spirit of fear, come to the
> forefront of all of the other unclean spirits. Fear and
> any of the fruit you have attempted to grow and
> seeds you have attempted to plant, you are cast out
> now, in the name of Jesus. Get out!*

You should experience some form of expulsion. If not, you
have not clearly identified the lid spirit. Be still and ask the Holy
Spirit the name of the lid spirit. Continue to name the stronghold
spirit and its fruit. Command them to come out. Allow the Holy
Spirit to give you the names of the fruit that needs to be removed.
You will want to ask the Holy Spirit to show you what is
happening with the unclean spirits inside of the temple. You
should experience an expulsion after every command. Here is
another example for you:

> *In Jesus' name, doubt. Get out now! Come up and come out
> now, never to return. Hesitation, get out now. Distraction,
> you are now cast out. Stress, get out now! Faithlessness, get
> out now, in the name of Jesus. Spirit of fear and all named or
> unnamed fruit that you have grown, get out now and never
> return! In Jesus' name.*

Here is an example of how you command the spirit of
infirmity.

> *In the name of Jesus, spirit of infirmity that has manifested in
> the form of _____ {name the sickness or diagnosis one-
> by-one} Get out! Spirit of infirmity or whatever stronghold*

spirit opened to door to the deceit of sickness in my body, in the name of Jesus.

I belong to Jesus and therefore, sickness can no longer be allowed to remain in my body. The unclean fruit named _____. Get out of my body right now in the name of Jesus' and you are never to return. You are not allowed to enter into any other people or objects in Jesus' name. Get out of my _____ (name the place where it has been manifesting such as your heart, right hip, head, stomach, etc.) this instant in the name of Jesus.

No more! This disease, discomfort, pain and unsteadiness ends this instant. My healing is complete and my healing is done, in Jesus' name, Amen.

Continue this until you have gotten through all of the strongholds and their fruits. Allow the Holy Spirit to tell you the names of additional fruit that may not have been on the lists I provided. This will become natural to you the moment you understand your position in the Heavenly rank.

This is where most deliverance ends, but you are not done yet. God has shown me an additional step that is required before the process is complete.

Chapter Ten

Calling In the Clean Spirits

After I was first delivered I felt oddly empty. I felt as if I was a balloon and the air was let out of me. I wanted to sleep. Then, I walked around in total bliss, joy, and feeling "out of sorts" for several days after the process. I knew that there had to be something I was missing. God continued to teach me that there was another step.

I was sitting on my couch one day feeling all warm and fuzzy inside and realized that I had no urge or drive to do any work whatsoever. Knowing that I still had a ministry to run, people to minister to, appointments to book and preaching to do, I knew I needed something more to be energized to continue the work.

I joyfully told God, "If I keep this up, I won't get anything done." I knew that there had to be an additional aspect of this work that was beyond anything I had read or studied.

Then, I heard God say, "You need more than my Holy Spirit to fully function. With the Holy Spirit you will have its fruit, but you need more to be grounded and do my will. Just as there are unclean fruits, there are more clean fruits you need. Just as you cast out the unclean, you must call in the clean."

I knew exactly what that meant. There were other clean spirits that produce other clean fruit that I needed in my life. That sent me on a study of all of the clean spirits in the Word. I also knew that just as there was a pattern of stronghold unclean spirits, there must be a hierarchy or order to the clean spirits. I prayed to God to show me.

It was only a few days later that I was sitting in a class that Apostle Forte was teaching and he began to teach about the Seven Spirits of God. While I knew that the number "seven" was significant in the Word, I had never fully understood that there were seven characteristics or spirits of God.

I knew in my spirit that this was the key! I knew that just as there were unclean stronghold spirits, there were seven clean spirits that each produced their own fruit. I began to ask Him questions as to which spirit governed which clean fruit. He unfolded a mighty teaching about money as a fruit of the Spirit of Wisdom that I shared on my CD *Moving The Mountain of Money*. Just after I completed charting the unclean fruit, I began to chart the clean fruit.

I was far outside of anything I had ever heard or read, so I had to rely solely on the Holy Spirit for the teachings. I received confirmation that the teachings were accurate because as soon as I began to apply the teaching, people moved past the feeling of being emptied out to being fulfilled. They began having an acute clarity of purpose and the natural desire to take action.

I went through every spirit in the Bible and asked the Holy Spirit to show me which of the seven spirits of God governed or produced which clean spirits. I am sharing here what He brought me. I also asked God to reveal to me the relationship between the Holy Spirit and the Seven Spirits of God.

The Holy Spirit

The Holy Spirit is the full expression of God. The fruit of the Holy Spirit are a result of all of the seven Spirits of God operating in your life. When you have the evidence of the seven Spirits of

God, you will produce the fruit (Gal 5:22) that represents total completion in God – The Holy Spirit.

When all seven of the Spirits of God are present in your life, you will be a living embodiment of the fruits of The Holy Spirit and you will live above the law. There are no more unclean spirits in your life. God will have fulfilled His prophetic word in Ezekiel 36:24-30, when he says that he will save you from your uncleanness. The human aspect of yourself has fully died and you are living as your divine Self.

The Seven Spirits of God and Their Fruit

Once you are done casting out, it is imperative that you now call in the clean spirits and command them to manifest in their clean fruit so you can operate in the fullness of God. When all of the seven spirits of God and their fruit manifest in your life you will then live in the full expression of God effortlessly producing the fruits of His Holy Spirit, love, joy, peace patience, kindness, goodness, faithfulness, gentleness and self-control (or sound mind).

> *And the spirit of the LORD shall rest upon him, the spirit of wisdom and understanding, the spirit of counsel and might, the spirit of knowledge and of the fear of the LORD – Isaiah 11:2*

The Seven Spirits of God are:

The Spirit of The Lord

The Spirit of Wisdom

The Spirit of Understanding

The Spirit of Counsel

The Spirit of Might

The Spirit of Knowledge

The Spirit of The Fear (Reverence) of The Lord

The Fruit of the Seven Spirits of God

The Spirit of The Lord

Rulership/Headship

Obedience

Kingdom

Spirit of adoption

Liberty

Freedom

Excellence/Excellent Spirit

Willing/Free

Authority

The Spirit of Wisdom

Favor

Financial stability

Wealth

Prosperity

Abundance

Clarity of vision

Ability to Hear the Holy Spirit Clearly

Revelation

Spirit of Grace and Supplications

Currency

Resources

The Spirit of Understanding

Spirit of My Understanding

Discernment

Faithful Spirit/Trustworthy

Gifts

Spirit of Meekness

The Spirit of Counsel

Service

Ministering Spirit

Spirit of Prophecy

The Spirit of Might

Workmanship

Sound Mind/Self-Discipline

Steadfast/Right Spirit

Power

Dominion

The Spirit of Knowledge

Information

Your Ability to Learn

Spirit of Revelation in the Knowledge of Him

The Spirit of The Fear (Reverence) of The Lord

Humility/Humble Spirit

Reverence

Spirit of Glory

While this list is a work in progress and requires more research, this list is sufficient in calling forth the spirits that you need to effectively walk out God's call on your life and manifest the fruits of the Holy Spirit. This process creates wholeness and completion to the work. Now you are walking in the fullness of God.

DECLARATION OF WHOLENESS

After the unclean stronghold spirits and their fruits have been expelled, here is an example of how you call in the Seven Spirits of God and their fruit.

Heavenly Father, in the name of Jesus, I stand on the truth of your word that states that I have been made whole by faith. I am a child of light and I am now separated from the darkness.

I now fully utilize the power, in the name of Jesus, that You have placed in my tongue to speak life and resurrect things that have died. In the name of Jesus, Spirit of The Lord, manifest in my life in a mighty way. By the power Jesus Christ has vested in my tongue, mind, body and spirit, re-align with my Heavenly Father's Rulership and Headship in my life. I yield my life to my Father's authority. I lay my life down at His feet so He may do with it what He has predestined.

In the name of Jesus, obedience, liberty, excellence and freedom to manifest in my life right now, in Jesus' name. I acknowledge that The Kingdom of God does not exist outside of me but within me. I now allow the will of Jesus to be done in my life as His Temple in which He built His Kingdom.

In the name of Jesus, Spirit of Adoption, come in and make it's home in my heart so I will always be fully connected to the profound love God has for me. From this day forward, I am filled with and connected to the love of my Heavenly Father at all times.

In the name of Jesus, Spirit of Wisdom, manifest mightily in favor, financial stability, wealth, prosperity, abundance and clarity of vision so I can live life and life more abundantly and truly prosper in my soul and every area of my life. My ears are now opened so I can hear what The Holy Spirit is saying to me and I can hear His revelation teachings and instructions clearly and concisely at all times and in all places. Spirit of grace and supplications, flow freely in my life. I will no longer wait for the provision before I move, I will move and know that My Father will bring forth the provision at the appointed time. In Jesus' name, Spirit of Wisdom, manifest in the form of the currency and money I need to walk out the fullness of the vision for which Jesus has set me aside.

The Spirit of Wisdom, create more than enough currency, more than enough time and more than enough wisdom to properly administer the gifts that have been bestowed upon me. The Word of God says that He will cause men to give into my bosom good measure, pressed down, shaken together, and running over. I receive it now, in the Jesus' name. I trust God to manifest as Jehovah Jirah, my provider. I open my heart and mind to all the Heavenly Father has for me and call forth who I know myself to be in the spirit to manifest even more powerfully in the natural.

In the name of Jesus, Spirit of Understanding, manifest in the discernment to recognize those who God has sent to forward His will and way in my life. Open up my spirit of understanding so I can be trusted with to complete the work My Heavenly Father created me to complete. Faithful spirit, grow and expand in me and make me trustworthy to bear the name of a Child of God. Spirit of meekness, manifest in my life so My Lord continues to open up His gifts in me so that I may go out and build His Kingdom on earth as it is in Heaven.

In the name of Jesus, Spirit of Counsel, plant yourself deeply in my temple so that I will always represent You to others through service. Ministering spirits of God, surround me, protect me and encamp around me so that I am protected from the wiles of the devil. Spirit of Prophecy, lead and guide me so I may always know the direction to go in to fulfill the vision God has for me, in the name of Jesus.

Spirit of Might, manifest in the workmanship that enables me to complete this calling on my life. Make yourself known in my life as a sound mind and self-discipline to put down all things of the flesh so that the adversary has no influence in my life whatsoever. Produce the fruits of a steadfast and right spirit with all of the power and dominion my Heavenly Father intended for me.

Spirit of Knowledge, you are now called forth in Jesus' name to produce the information needed to move the learning of the things of God within me so that I continue to remain in my rightful position above the laws of this world. Show yourself powerfully as the spirit of revelation in the knowledge of my Lord and Savior.

In the name of Jesus, Spirit of The Reverence of the Lord, manifest in my life so that the glory of God is demonstrated at all times, with humility and devotion to the ways of God, without hesitation or hindrance from this instant and for the rest of my life.

From this day forward, my light shines before men and draws men unto Jesus. I receive from the men you are sending to me to assist me in fulfilling your purpose for my life. I now move in the fullness of the abundant, prosperous, and healthy life you have called me to live with every need met by the riches of my Father. I receive the life My Heavenly Father has for me that exceeds anything I can even think or imagine. I will be most careful to give you all the praise, honor and glory. In Jesus' name. Amen.

Praise God!!! You should be on your feet praising and worshipping God. He has fully recreated and restored you to your original splendor! To God be the glory!

Now that you are cleaned in your heart and spirit and have allowed your body time to recalibrate, you must begin to walk in the fullness of your calling. Be the vessel through which Jesus can now continue this work in others. With this work, it is possible to change the entire Body of Christ as we know it.

Chapter Eleven

No More Sickness

There is something I just have to reiterate to make sure you fully understand the Truth. While I mentioned it earlier in the book, because God desires to move among His people with greater signs and wonders in the days to come, you must get this teaching down into your very core.

As you fully lay down your life in exchange for the one Jesus has for you, a natural part of that process is for you to be without sickness and disease. As I was praying and asking God to teach me about this work, I knew that deliverance and healing were directly related. I asked Him, "God, which comes first, the healing or the deliverance." He answered, "Look in the Word." It did not take long to notice that deliverance always occurred before healing. As I mentioned earlier, healing is actually a *result* of deliverance.

I need an entire *Physician's Desk Reference* to list out the seemingly endless manifestations of the spirit of infirmity. There are so many that it is difficult to even wrap your mind around the fact that *all* sickness is a form of an unclean spirit. While God sometimes allows an unclean spirit of sickness or infirmity to exist waiting to see if you will use the opportunity to stand in the authority He has placed in your tongue and cast out the sickness to His glory, it still originates from an unclean spirit.

The medical industry has to continually add new diseases and possible treatments to keep up with Satan's attack on your body – the temple of God. No matter how much confidence you have in the medical field, there are no exceptions to sickness being of Satan.

I know that the medical field is critical for those of the world, but it should not be necessary for believers if we understood early enough what was really going on. But because we have been blinded to the truth, it is and has been quite necessary to turn to the medical field and prescriptions to work with the sickness that has manifested in our temples.

There are no exceptions to sickness being of Satan.

Even if God is allowing the sickness for His glory, it is Him allowing the unclean spirit to manifest so He can show His glory in the healing. When you think of every hospital around the world with all of the infirm people who are at various stages of sickness, it paints the picture of just how successful Satan has been in attempting to keep you from your power in Christ.

This stronghold spirit of infirmity has definitely permeated the Church. Everyday we are losing congregants, pastors, first ladies, ministers, ushers, elders and deacons. I am going on the record to say that we lose them because of our lack of belief and understanding of the position we occupy in the heavenly realm as believers.

Just last week I received an email from Rachel, a believer who enrolled in one of my upcoming workshops. She would be unable to make it to the workshop because she was in a Washington DC area hospital visiting her sick father. She sounded sad on the phone and I knew that her father must not have been doing well. I told her that I would be praying for her father.

I was sitting there thinking to myself, "Should I call her and tell her that she has been granted the power over her father's sickness through Jesus?" I did not actually call her because I haven't had the chance to know where she is in her walk with God and you have to know how to move in this realm when you begin taking your rightful place above Satan.

Instead, I was even more focused on completing this book and getting it into her hands, so she could have a full understanding that her father does not have to die. At the leading of the Holy Spirit, she has the power, through Jesus, to literally heal him and call him back from the dead no matter what happened within the walls of that hospital.

We have been losing this battle for far too long and it is time to get back in our rightful place through Christ Jesus. I could not finish this book without making sure you fully understand the power you have over all sickness and disease as a child of God.

> We have been losing this battle for far too long and it is time to get back in our rightful place through Christ Jesus.

We demonstrate the knowledge of who we are in Christ through speaking the Truth and applying the power of our tongues, which literally holds life and death. We are constantly speaking life or death and the fruit of what we are speaking is evident in our lives (Proverbs 18:21).

I can almost hear you asking, "So, Ericka...are you saying that no Christian is ever supposed to die?" God designed the human body to live to be one-hundred twenty years old. So, I'll let you draw your own conclusions. Satan was granted power over sin and death and he has been defeated (Hebrews 2:14). The Word clearly says that the wages of sin are death (Romans 6:23).

> *He who does what is sinful is of the devil, because the devil has been sinning from the beginning. The reason the Son of God appeared was to destroy the devil's work. - IJohn 3:8*

When I was beginning to wrap my mind around this, I had to stop and think of just how many people die as a result of sin – either their sin or the sin of others - and it is Satan's unclean spirits that lead us to sin. The answer is far too many.

I do know that those who truly live for God and walk with Him will not die; they are promised everlasting and eternal life.

> *"I tell you the truth, whoever hears my word and believes him who sent me has eternal life and will not be condemned; he has crossed over from death to life.*
> *– John 5:24*

This means that believers are supposed to be transcribed into Heaven to walk with God and not to die from any sickness, accident or other form or fashion. I'm sure this is opening up a potential debate and it is one that God fully addresses in His word. That really leaves only one question, "Is your faith big enough to believe it?"

Is your faith big enough to believe it?

A PRAYER FOR YOU

Father, in the name of Jesus, I thank you for bearing the_ so I do not have to. I thank you for giving your life so that I might live without sickness. Thank you that above all things you intend for me to prosper and be in good health as my soul prospers.

Lord, I come to you confessing that I have not had the faith enough to believe that you are Jehovah- Rophe, the Lord Who Heals. Father, today is the day that I get to know you as the God of healing. Your Word says that whatever I ask in your name, it will be given to me. In Jesus' name, I stand in my full power, authority, and dominion over the spirit of infirmity and all of the sickness and disease it has created in my body – the temple of the Lord.

No matter what I have done in the past or how I have treated this temple of God, I declare it as Holy Ground today. Satan, you have no place or rights to this Holy Ground. You will get out of my body and you will never return. You will leave quickly and without leaving damage behind, in Jesus' name.

Father, in the name of Jesus, I am standing on the truth of your word that says by your stripes, I am healed. I stand on the Truth of your Word that says, "It is done." Therefore, I am healed and from this instant forward I have no more pain or symptoms of sickness or disease. I am healed. I am whole. I am complete. I am free to walk out your will with no pain and without anything that is cast out today ever returning again for the rest of my life. In Jesus' name. Amen.

Chapter Twelve

Your Will and His Will Become One

The only thing left once you have realigned yourself with the Truth of who you are in Jesus, cleansed your heart of unforgiveness and your spirit of unclean spirits is for you to be completely free for God's use and exaltation.

Before my complete deliverance I used to ask God each and everyday, "Lord, what would you have me to do today?" While I have a business background and often know what I *could* do to move my ministry forward, I learned early on that the only things that worked successfully were the things that God instructed me to do. Anything else failed and went into the "it was a good lesson learned" pile. So I made it a habit to check my every move with God.

While I always wrote out my 'to-do list and scheduled my time accordingly, doing what I thought I should do and what God would have me do were two different things at that point in my walk. To my surprise, after He cleaned me, one morning I was inquiring as to what He would have me do in the ministry that day and I heard," You are now clean. I can fully trust you. You are free to do those things that you already know to do."

I just sat there taking it in. I had this image in my mind of a horse in the starting gates before a big race and the moment the gate opens up for the horse to run the race freely. I knew God was telling me that I was free to run. He could trust me. There was no unclean thing left in me and therefore I was finally, truly filled with Him. There was no "me" left. I truly believe that this is what the Word means by being born again.

---

*I truly believe that this is what the Word means
by being born again.*

God did not intend for His people to carry both His Holy Spirit *and* unclean spirits. To belong fully to Jesus, you must fully carry *only* His spirit and fruit. To be filled means to have no space for anything else. You cannot be truly born again until you have no unclean thing left within you and are filled entirely with the Holy Spirit. God did not intend for you to have both unclean and clean spirits; to be partially of Heaven and partially of the world. You are to belong entirely to God, which means that you have to carry *only* the Holy Spirit and the Seven Spirits of God. Through this work I have learned that *having* the Holy Spirit and being *filled* with the Holy Spirit are two different things. Until every believer goes through each step God shared in this book, they are not *filled* with The Holy Spirit. They are only partially experiencing or have the Holy Spirit.

I know...that one almost knocked the wind out of you, right?

The Clarity of The Lord

Every person Jesus has guided in deliverance through me has reported an intense clarity of purpose from the Lord. Once he or she is done recalibrating, that person wakes up one morning fully able to see their clear path to living God's vision for his or her life. I use the analogy of what it must feel like to be an airplane pilot. Yes, you can use the instruments to guide your way to see through the fog of the unclean, but on a clear day, you can see your purpose for miles.

The clarity that you have is amazing! It is so amazing that I have created a whole, new program just for those who have been cleansed. You no longer have the same issues as everyone else. Where you were not sure of what to do to move forward before deliverance, you are clear and have no resistance whatsoever after deliverance. All that is left is to prioritize all of the instructions God is pouring into you.

No More Pushing

One very distinct part of the new reality of being delivered and cleansed is that you no longer have to push. You no longer experience struggle and that constant pushing against the brick wall of your life to try to move forward. The way is opened and you can casually walk through without shoving your way forward. You have entered into the flow of God. God will now fully open His "blueprint" for your life to you.

Accessing Your Inner Blue Print

God planted a blueprint within you that holds every direction, resource, instruction and revelation you need to fully manifest His vision for your life. Just like the clouds clearing out of the way of a lovely blue sky on a rainy day, once you are cleansed you can see your inner blueprint.

It is like the overgrown brush has been moved out of the way to a path that has been there all along. Now you only have to take steps to move in the direction of your destiny.

Make sure you keep a notebook with you at all times, (I even take mine with me in the bathroom) because you never know where God will open some instruction or revelation in you. It begins to come so fast that you will have to write it down to keep up.

Allow God to unfold Himself to you even more. This requires more time in the Word, prayer, meditation, and fasting. You must create new patterns of behavior because your old patterns, based upon managing your previous unclean spirits, are no longer effective. Your old patterns will not serve you as you move forward. Your old behaviors are no longer relevant to your future walk with God. Creating new patterns begins with mastering your environment.

Mastering Your Environment

At my retreats, all of the participants gather for the last session on Sunday morning. They have all been fully delivered and have the same burning question, "Now what?" Now that they were cleansed, how do they go back into the very life that was created in conjunction with the unclean spirits that were residing within them?

You must really understand that *all* unclean spirits are subject to you, through Jesus, and that includes those that others people are carrying. Now that you have commanded the unclean spirits that were in you, you must command the unclean spirits that are in others.

> You must really understand that all unclean spirits are subject to you, through Jesus, and that includes those that others people are carrying.

The first thing to do is to get your environment into submission. Begin with your home, your family, your body, and your habits. You have to create a new pattern by which to live. The old one does not fit anymore. When you look around your life, you will have outgrown it like a pair of jeans that are too tight. You might be able to squeeze into them, but they will not be comfortable to move in.

Yet, you still have the same house, the same kids, spouse, job and car. You may find yourself looking around your life feeling like you just don't fit there anymore – it no longer fits who you are.

You first need to assess the specific areas that no longer fit who you now are in Christ. It may mean setting aside time to clean your physical space, have a family meeting to lay down new guidelines and boundaries, or a private meeting with your spouse to share what you really need in this new space.

It may not be easy, but you must take authority and create new patterns in your life. This is about taking the land so you can move into God's Promised Land. You will uncover the next steps to move forward in your answers to these questions:

-

- What no longer works for you?
- What do you need to be fully supported in your new life?
- What habits and behaviors need to go?
- What relationships no longer fit?
- What do you need to communicate to those around you about your new reality?

Begin taking action on your answers as you deal with the unclean spirits of those in your life.

Affecting Those Around You

Now that you understand how stronghold spirits manifest, you will be able to recognize the presence and know the names of the unclean spirits in the lives of those around you. It is now time to cast them down. It is important not to pass judgment on people, but to allow the Holy Spirit to compassionately guide you in helping others who are oppressed. It is not your place to judge, leave that to God.

You now recognize that before, you thought your boss was just perpetually in a bad mood. Now you see that he or she is carrying the spirit of jealousy and lying spirit. Maybe you thought that your spouse was just negative and unable to support you before, but now you recognize that he or she is being oppressed by the spirit of heaviness and perverse spirit.

Perhaps you thought that your child's teacher was just evil and had no patience for children. Now you can clearly see that they are carrying the spirit of whoredoms and are in constant physical pain by lying spirit and the spirit of infirmity. Perhaps you are now noticing that your co-workers curse a lot and you did not notice before.

Your spiritual eyes and ears are now opened and there is no turning back. It is time to realize that your dominion, authority and power of unclean spirits goes far beyond only you. You have been granted the power to cast down spirits in those around you.

While you cannot cast out their unclean spirits without them granting you that authority in their life, you can cast them down so they are not allowed to manifest through other people in your life and the lives of those you love in your presence or as commanded. Their unclean spirits – whether they are saved or not – must obey the name of Jesus.

You must now take authority over the people and places in your surroundings, beginning with your home. If your family or whomever you live with is demonstrating any unclean fruit, you must cast that fruit down and insist that it no longer enters your home or manifests in your loved one or whomever you may live with. If you have a spouse that is not supportive or is not a reflection of the fruits of The Holy Spirit, then it is time for you to speak directly to his or her unclean spirits and subdue them.

Once you have taken back your home, then it is time to take back your space at your job. I have worked with several people who were outstanding employees and threatened their insecure managers and co-workers and had become the object of attack in their workplace. While everyone else they came in contact with said their work was stellar, their power was too threatening (spirit of jealousy) for their insecure (spirit of whoredoms) managers and their managers began lying (lying spirit) on them to get them fired. Two clients who came to me were actually scheduled for disciplinary hearings the following week at their jobs.

After they learned that the unclean spirits operating in their bosses and co-workers cannot stand against their authority they spoke directly to the unclean spirits, in Jesus' name, and let them know that they are no longer allowed to manifest through their bosses, coworkers or anyone else in the work place.

They both had supernatural turnarounds at their jobs and are now enjoying peaceful and supportive work environments. They were both amazed at how easy and effective it was the moment they realized that the unclean spirits in their bosses and coworkers are subject to their authority in Jesus.

This work is effective in any area of your life. I have actually cast down unclean spirits in my former church and within a matter of hours, the person carrying them left the church. Although that is not what I asked for, it is how God took care of it. Apply these teachings to your home, job, church, child's school and anywhere else your feet touch throughout your life. You can see an example of commanding or casting down unclean spirits in the prayers and declarations at the end of this chapter. I am serious about no unclean thing being allowed to show up in my life.

Take time to answer the following questions so you are clear about what those around you are dealing with:

- What unclean spirits can you recognize in your loved ones?

- Your coworkers?

- Your church family?

What to Expect in Your New Life

There is something I need to warn you about. I have to give you fair warning that there may be people in your life who don't know what do with the new you. Those who are still oppressed with unclean spirits will not be able to come into your presence. Because you have cast down any unclean spirits from coming near you, the unclean spirits still living within those people have to obey.

You will notice that people will no longer be able to look you in the eye. Your invitations to casual gatherings may dwindle and those who can't hang will just keep their distance. It can actually be quite comical when you think about it. I have witnessed people actually running from me since my deliverance. You will now make unclean spirits uncomfortable.

Be careful not to take it personally. It is just God setting you apart. But you do want to be aware of it so you do not feel too isolated. I always suggest that people share their experience with someone who is in similar place in their walk with God and will want to also experience being cleansed, so you all can connect at the new level.

Those who are in your life and are ready for the work will begin to comment on how something is different about you and ask you what happened to you. That is an opening and sign that they are ready for the work themselves and would love to learn more about your process and experience. Make sure you share it with them.

Other people who have been delivered will also appear and want to connect with you. Like spirits are attracted to like spirits. It is a wonderful opportunity to forge new friendships with people who are trustworthy and of like spirit and mind. Enjoy the process of moving to a new altitude in your relationships.

I have created gatherings and tele-classes for those who no longer have issues in their life due to their deliverance and cleansing. Feel free to find opportunities to connect on my website, www.erickajackson.com.

The Possibilities

When you truly grasp the possibilities of this work, it is massive. Understanding the many, many ways that Satan uses his unclean spirits to oppress and control our lives and that there is a way to stop it. This means that we can take back our families, our communities and end so many of the world's issues and shortcomings.

Not only can you take dominion over your life, but you can assist others in taking dominion over theirs. This work has the power to clean out entire churches, communities and nations. God has given you the power to cast out one thousand demons and with two people on one accord, you can cast out ten thousand (Deuteronomy 32:30). Imagine what we could do with several people who understand their Heavenly rank and are on one accord. Once your way is clear from unclean spirits, there is nothing you cannot do with Jesus.

Allow yourself to embrace the possibilities of what you can do as you bring forth God's vision for your life. You have everything you need right now. You lack nothing. Now, go and do what God has called you to do. BE who God called you to be. You are free to walk in the fullness of God and all of the freedom and liberty He has set aside especially for you.

Beloved, I wish above all things that you may prosper and be in health, even as thy soul prospers. – 3 John 1:2

A DECLARATION TO YOUR SURROUNDINGS

Heavenly Father, in the name of Jesus, thank you for being such an awesome and mighty God. Thank you for granting me the power to do all things through Christ who strengthens me. Thank you for raising me up and placing me at the right hand of Jesus and therefore giving me the power, dominion and authority over all things in the spiritual realm and all things in the natural realm. Thank you for blessing me with the power to subdue the earth and everything in it.

Right now, the fullness of this power and my position in the heavenly rank are loosed ,in the name of Jesus. Satan is subject to the name of Jesus and must obey every command Jesus authorized me to speak. He has no real power over me, my decisions, my belongings, my body, my mind, my spirit or any aspect of me or my life.

Today, right this instant, I decree and declare myself and everything that comes in contact with me as Holy Ground, and therefore, Satan, you have no jurisdiction or authority over me or anything I come in contact with at any time and in any way. I am a co-heir with Christ and I will be fully obedient and persevere to obtain my full inheritance, you will no longer cause me to hesitate or fall short of who I am in Christ.

I stand on the Word of God that says that whatever I bind on earth will be bound in Heaven and whatever I loose on earth shall be loosed in Heaven. Satan and every unclean thing you have attempted to loose in my life is now bound to the Word of God that says that you have been defeated and that nothing is impossible with God.

With all of the power, authority, wisdom and dominion granted me through Christ Jesus, Satan, your influence and your unclean spirits are now off of my life, my family, my friends, my belongings and any and everything in my surroundings. You have no access to my electronics, my vehicle and any other tools that God has given to me to fulfill His call in my life. They are Holy Ground and have been consecrated for God's use and purpose. Any doors I have unknowingly left open for you to gain access to the tools in my life are now closed and you are locked out forever, never to return in Jesus' name.

In Jesus' name, no unclean spirit – whether named or unnamed – is allowed to manifest in anyone I know, anyone I come in contact with, or anyone I even cross paths with for any amount of time. Satan, you are not allowed to use anyone to speak against me, my name, or my work from this instant forward. In the name of Jesus, no one is allowed to even mention my name negatively and when they may attempt to do so, Holy Spirit bind their lips, so they cannot say anything against me, a child of the Most High God.

In the name of Jesus, Satan, you will no longer even attempt to use my spouse, family, friends or acquaintances to speak anything against the work God has called me to do. Lying Spirit, you will never again manifest or attempt to influence me against who I know myself to be in Christ ever again. I am whole, complete and now know I sit at the right hand of Jesus above all rule, authority and powers of this world. All things in the natural real and the spiritual realm are under my fee. In the name of Jesus. Amen.

A FINAL DECLARATION FOR YOU

Father, in the name of Jesus, In the presence of my Heavenly Father and all things in the spiritual realms and the natural world, I boldly come to the throne of God declaring that from this day forward every moment of my life will fully represent the glory of God and nothing will get in the way. I am who God says I am and I will do what God has called me to do.

In the name of Jesus, I now easily move in the will of God in my life each and every day. People, money, resources, wealth, knowledge and the information that is needed to fully manifest God's vision for my life now appear with ease and with the grace of God.

In the name of Jesus, I speak life into every aspect of my being and into the lives of those around me. I love Jesus Christ, my Lord and Savior, with all of my heart, spirit and soul and nothing or no one will ever be allowed to slow or stop the full manifestation of God in my life. I am a beacon of light for God and shine as brightly as He would have me shine from this day forward so men can be drawn to Jesus through me and my life.

In the name of Jesus, I now take my rightful place in the heavenly rank and remember from this day forward that God has placed me above all spiritual things and all natural things, in Jesus' name. Father God, manifest the fruit of Your Holy Spirit in my life now, in Jesus' name. In Jesus' name, love, joy, peace, patience, kindness, goodness, faithfulness, gentleness and self-control, against which there is no law. Father God, I will be most careful to give you all the praise and all the glory forever and ever. In Jesus' name. Amen.

Those that the Son sets free are free indeed. Now, go live the life Jesus created you to live. Be who He created you to be. I love you and I wish the blessings of your Father in Heaven to rain down upon you from this day forward. With all my heart, Ericka.

With this in mind, we constantly pray for you, that our God may count you worthy of his calling, and that by His power He may fulfill every good purpose of your and every act prompted by your faith. We pray this so that the name of our Lord Jesus may be glorified in you, and you in Him, according to the grace of our God and the Lord Jesus Christ. – 2 Thes 1:11 – 12

Scripture References for Further Study

I have listed additional scripture references not already mentioned throughout the book for your further study. It is my prayer that these scriptures take you from knowledge to understanding and from understanding to evidence, from this day forward, so you can walk in the fullness of who you are in Christ every moment of the rest of your life.

May the Lord God open your spiritual eyes and uncover your spiritual ears so that you may hear what He intended the moment He had these scriptures written. He who has an ear, let him hear what the Spirit is saying. In Jesus' name. Amen.

Leviticus 26: 6 – 8	Matthew 8:28-32
Deuteronomy 18:9-15	Matthew 10:7-8
Deuteronomy 32:30	Matthew 12:43-45
Joshua 23:10	Matthew 16:18-19
II Kings 17:37-38	Matthew 18:19
Psalm 23:4	Matthew 28:18-20
Psalm 34:4	Mark 1:21; 23-25
Psalm 51:10	Mark 3:11
Psalm 139:23 – 24	Mark 9:25; 29
Proverbs 5:22	Mark 11:17-24
Proverbs 11:13	Mark 16:17-18
Proverbs 29:25	Luke 1:37
Isaiah 43:26	Luke 4:33-34
Ezekiel 11:19	Luke 4:41
Ezekiel 18:31	Luke 8:26-39
Joel 2:25	Luke 10:17-20
Joel 2:32	Luke 11:13
Matthew 4:9-10	Luke 11:24-26
Matthew 8:26	John 3:3

John 3:16-21
John 8:34
John 14:13-14; 17
John 15:1 - 7
John 16:23-24
John 20:22
Acts 2:17 – 19
Acts 8:7
Acts 8:23
Acts 19:12
Acts 26:17-18
Romans 7:6
Romans 7:22-25
Romans 8:9
I Corinthians 2:14
I Corinthians 6:19-20
II Corinthians 3:3
II Corinthians 3:18
II Corinthians 4:3-4
II Corinthians 10:3-5
Galatians 5:16-17
Galatians 6:1-2

Ephesians 1:13-14
Ephesians 2:1-2
Ephesians 4:20 – 24
Ephesians 6:10-18
Philippians 1:19
Philippians 4:8-9
Colossians 2:18-19
I Timothy 4:1
I Timothy 5:22
II Timothy 2:15
II Timothy 2:25-26
Hebrews 1:13-14
Hebrews 4:16
Hebrews 9:14
James 1:22-25
James 5:14-16
II Peter 2:19
I John 3:8
I John 4:18
I John 5:11-12
Revelation 16:14

Other Resources by Ericka D. Jackson

BOOKS

The Power of Vision

The Fearless Living Challenge

When God Calls

Self-Coaching

CD's

Baggage Free! Releasing Emotional Baggage

Creating Order

End Your Cash Crunch Now

Fear No More

Free Your Mind

Freedom From Fear

It's Time For A Schedule Tune-up

Moving The Mountain of Money

The Realm of The Impossible

Where Do I Begin?

And many speaking engagement recordings

SELF-STUDY COURSES

Free The Book Inside of You

Ministry Mastery: How to Create A Thriving Full-time Ministry

The Coaches' Call: Christian Coaches' Mentoring Program

BLOG

Visit Ericka's blog for revelation and Truth of God,
www.erickadjackson.wordpress.com

Visit www.erickajackson.com for ordering and to explore the articles and complimentary tools Ericka has created for you.

The Beyond Fearless Institute™

God has given me the commission to get this work out to the Body of Christ in a mighty way. I am putting together a ministerial team to train to take this work to believers around the world. If you are drawn to this work and know you are called to be a vessel for deliverance and healing, you may be interested in becoming one of our certified Beyond Fearless™ Trained Ministers to go out and take this work into the Body of Christ. For more information on *The Beyond Fearless Institute*™, visit www.erickajackson.com or email us at info@erickajackson.com.

References

Garrison, Mary, How to Try A Spirit: By Their Fruits You Will Know Them, Christ Camp Ministries, Inc. ©1976.

Hammond, Frank and Ida Mae, *Pigs in The Parlor: A Practical Guide to Deliverance*, Impact Christian Books, © 1970.

The Holy Spirit.